Cambridge Elements

Elements in Language Teaching
edited by
Heath Rose
University of Oxford
Jim McKinley
University College London

LANGUAGE LEARNING BEYOND ENGLISH

Learner Motivation in the Twenty-First Century

Ursula Lanvers
University of York

Shaftesbury Road, Cambridge CB2 8EA, United Kingdom

One Liberty Plaza, 20th Floor, New York, NY 10006, USA

477 Williamstown Road, Port Melbourne, VIC 3207, Australia

314–321, 3rd Floor, Plot 3, Splendor Forum, Jasola District Centre, New Delhi – 110025, India

103 Penang Road, #05–06/07, Visioncrest Commercial, Singapore 238467

Cambridge University Press is part of Cambridge University Press & Assessment, a department of the University of Cambridge.

We share the University's mission to contribute to society through the pursuit of education, learning and research at the highest international levels of excellence.

www.cambridge.org
Information on this title: www.cambridge.org/9781009486958

DOI: 10.1017/9781009388795

© Ursula Lanvers 2024

This publication is in copyright. Subject to statutory exception and to the provisions of relevant collective licensing agreements, with the exception of the Creative Commons version the link for which is provided below, no reproduction of any part may take place without the written permission of Cambridge University Press & Assessment.

An online version of this work is published at doi.org/10.1017/9781009388795 under a Creative Commons Open Access license CC-BY-NC 4.0 which permits re-use, distribution and reproduction in any medium for non-commercial purposes providing appropriate credit to the original work is given and any changes made are indicated. To view a copy of this license visit https://creativecommons.org/licenses/by-nc/4.0

When citing this work, please include a reference to the DOI 10.1017/9781009388795

First published 2024

A catalogue record for this publication is available from the British Library.

ISBN 978-1-009-48695-8 Hardback
ISBN 978-1-009-38881-8 Paperback
ISSN 2632-4415 (online)
ISSN 2632-4407 (print)

Additional resources for this publication at www.cambridge.org/Lanvers

Cambridge University Press & Assessment has no responsibility for the persistence or accuracy of URLs for external or third-party internet websites referred to in this publication and does not guarantee that any content on such websites is, or will remain, accurate or appropriate.

Language Learning beyond English

Learner Motivation in the Twenty-First Century

Elements in Language Teaching

DOI: 10.1017/9781009388795
First published online: June 2024

Ursula Lanvers
University of York

Author for correspondence: Ursula Lanvers, ursula.lanvers@york.ac.uk

Abstract: This Element addresses the following three questions: can Global English unequivocally be framed as a 'killer' language for learning LOTEs (languages other than English)? If so, under what premises? (Section 1); what are the rationales and justifications for learning LOTE in the age of Global English? (Section 2); and what are the pedagogical and policy implications for learning LOTE in the age of Global English? What can we learn from current (best and less good) practice? (Section 3). Attempts to engage learners in learning a variety of languages – rather than just English – often fail to achieve desired results, in both anglophone and non-anglophone contexts. Can English be blamed? What can policymakers and educators do to address the crisis? This Element proposes a new matrix of rationales for language learning, advocating an interconnected, socially embedded justification for language learning. This title is also available as Open Access on Cambridge Core.

Keywords: language policy, language education policy, motivation research, rationales for language education, holistic education

© Ursula Lanvers 2024

ISBNs: 9781009486958 (HB), 9781009388818 (PB), 9781009388795 (OC)
ISSNs: 2632-4415 (online), 2632-4407 (print)

Contents

1 Introduction   1

2 Framing English as a Killer Language   22

3 Rationales for Language Learning: A Twenty-First Century Matrix   31

4 Harnessing Rationales to Foster Motivation: Meeting Learners' Needs   47

5 Conclusion   61

References   64

Supplementary materials are available to access at www.cambridge.org/Lanvers

1 Introduction

Wer fremde Sprachen nicht kennt, weiß nichts von seiner Eigenen. People who know no foreign languages know nothing of their own. This has been replaced by a third global English myth, namely that in international communication the only language you need is English, as expressed in my update of Goethe's maxim: Wer Englisch kennt, braucht keine anderen Sprachen. Whoever knows English has no need of other languages.

(Phillipson 2017a: 317)

1.1 Scope of the Element

This Element addresses the challenges Global English poses to the formal (School) learning of languages other than English (LOTE). As Global English is continuing to change our language learning landscape, policymakers, educators and learners themselves need to adapt to the sometimes unpalatable reality that one language seems, to many learners, more desirable to learn than any other (de Swaan, 2001a). Globally, many language education systems continue to be marked by English displacing other languages hitherto used (Englishisation), while targets for LOTE learning are not achieved. Mass migration and increasing societal multilingualism in a wide range of LOTE further add to an increasing mismatch between official language education policy (LEP) and sociopolitical needs for language skills. Language education policy planning and school provision remain ill equipped to respond to the challenging needs for a twenty-first century education (Kramsch, 2014; Pachler, 2002).

While international organisations subscribe to equality of all languages (Council of Europe, 2020; UNESCO, n.d.), the Englishisation of education systems continues (e.g. Wilkinson & Gabriëls, 2021a). Recently, the discipline of applied linguistics has undergone radical paradigm shifts advocating equality in language learning and language use, most importantly the multilingual turn (May, 2019) and the translanguaging turn (García & Wei, 2014). Meanwhile, the undeniable preference for the learning of English over LOTE has received comparatively less attention (Lanvers et al., 2021a). Thus, as modern paradigms in applied linguistics strive for ever more equity between languages, and in language use, breaking disciplinary and language boundaries (Wei, 2020), language learning preferences and uptake patterns remain unaffected. We observe a growing gap between the conceptual developments in applied linguistics and language policy on the one hand, and practices of language learning on the other (Gazzola, 2023).

This Element addresses these widening gaps in a two-pronged approach. First, it revisits traditional rationales for language learning, reframing them in a new scheme that emphasises non-material justifications for language study more than past rationales. This *holistic* matrix of rationales is designed to support educators and policymakers in designing and formulating their own language policy in the most comprehensive manner possible. In a novel departure, the matrix of rationales proposed here consists of two continuum dimensions:

Who benefits from language learning (individual or society)?
What is the nature of the benefit (material or non-material)?

The Element then undertakes the exacting task of connecting such rationales to our – by now, considerable – knowledge about language learner motivation. Although the twenty-first century has seen some conceptual contributions on the topic of rationales for language learning, it remains somewhat undertheorised. Rationales have also rarely, if at all, been linked to learner motivation, a striking lacuna since official rationales for LEP might be utilised to help learners understand the relevance of their endeavour. The second argument of the Element is that rationales *can* indeed be used to help motivate learners, provided that two conditions are met: they are explicitly communicated to, and discussed with, learners, and rationales are tailored to the basic human motivational needs of learners engaged in language study.

By preference, official rationales for language learning should help motivate learners. Despite a prolific literature on language learner motivation, the relation between rationales and motivation has hardly been investigated. The reason for this lacuna is that they operate at different levels: while rationales are logically conceptualised by policymakers, motivation sits (largely) at the experiential level of the individual. The best rationale for language learning could not compensate for a learner's experience of boredom in the classroom. Nonetheless, rational arguments for language learning have been used as motivational incentivisation in intervention studies. The online supplement to this Element (available at www.cambridge.org/lanvers) offers practical activities and methods designed to *incentivise non-material motivation for language learning*. In this sense, this Element bridges LEP research, language learning motivation research and pedagogical practice.

This Introduction sets out the incentive and context of the Element. Beyond, the Element is structured as follows: Section 2 asks under what conditions English might be framed as a threat to learning LOTE. Three conceptualisations of global language systems are discussed, and each system is scrutinised for the light it can shed on the question of what rationales might remain for the study of LOTE. The section concludes that, irrespective of whether English dominance in language learning is considered desirable, inevitable or harmful, language learning and teaching models conceptualising different language skills and their purposes as discrete neglect important recent paradigm shifts in applied linguistics, namely the multilingual turn and the translanguaging turn in language learning.

Section 3 first discusses the existing literature on rationales for formal language education and then presents a novel, two-dimensional matrix model of rationales for teaching foreign languages. This matrix, it is argued, can help policymakers, educators and learners themselves in reflecting on and formulating their specific motivation for language study, adapted to their contexts. Rationales for any formal language study have, hitherto, been under-theorised and often perform justificatory functions, defending policy rather than serving as a nexus from which curricula, schemes of work, pedagogies and so forth may emerge. The holistic matrix provided here is designed to help policymakers to formulate their rationales in the most holistic way possible for their context, and to communicate these better to stakeholders.

Section 4 undertakes the delicate translation from rationales to motivations. Putting rationales into the service of motivating learners is subject to many caveats, as many motivational factors, such as liking the teacher, lie outside the conceptual and logical remit of rationales. Nonetheless, some rationales overlap with motivational dimensions, and forms of incentivisation relating to this nexus remain underutilised to date. There is evidence that if rational incentivisation is targeted to specific learner groups and their specific motivational needs, it can have positive motivational effects. In other words, Section 4 puts the matrix into the service of motivating learners. Section 5 pulls together these different strings and discusses how we might best protect the learning of a diversity of languages in the future.

1.2 A Personal Professional Trajectory

If the world 'stampedes' towards the one language with the highest prestige while neglecting others, it might suggest that many learners share a somewhat asymmetrical motivational orientation, one that lacks appreciation of non-material, especially personal non-material rationales and benefits of language learning. The by now considerable wealth of empirical studies on language learner motivation underscores this observation. This global challenge in language learning has directed my attention towards rationales, questioning more closely *why* we make students learn foreign languages. Too often, in my experience as a secondary school language teacher in the UK, the legitimate student question *But why should we learn this?* has remained poorly addressed, if at all. The language learning crisis, triggered by Global English, has incentivised me to rethink rationales for language study more thoroughly, but the fundamental claims of (1) conceptualising all rationales holistically, with equal validity, and (2) connecting rationales to motivation reach far beyond this problem.

This Element also provides a reflection on the stages of my own involvement in language learning: from a somewhat 'rebellious' learner, preferring French to English as foreign language, to a teacher struggling with low student motivation, to a researcher focusing on student motivation, to a researcher focusing on education policies and global language trends, in order to finally realise the interconnectedness of these. Thus, to the extent that this Element interweaves empirical research with my personal trajectory, it is empirically grounded, but such 'joining of the dots' has also led me to a conceptual contribution concerning the nature of rationales for language learning, and the connectedness between rationales and motivation.

1.3 What Is Language Education Policy?

A traditional critical sociolinguistic approach to LEP views policy as 'one mechanism by which dominant groups establish hegemony in language use' (Tollefson, 1991: 16), thus enabling dominant groups to shape language practices in alignment with their ideology (Shohamy, 2016). This conceptualisation of LEP stresses the hegemonic power dynamics of institutions shaping participant behaviours. In this view, (lack of) equity in LEP might be gauged by the extent key stakeholders are involved in policymaking (Tollefson, 1991: 211). Language education policy can be officially declared in ratified documents and practised at the level of educational institutions and the individual, as well as debated and contested. Language education policies are always created in their politico-ideological contexts (Kramsch, 2005). Different metaphors have been applied to describe the multilayeredness of LEP, the best known being Ricento and Hornerger's (1996) onion metaphor; other descriptors include top-down versus bottom-up, implicit versus explicit, de jure versus de facto.

More recent theoretical contributions to language policy stress how policy is enacted, co-created and negotiated at all levels: the macro, meso and micro-levels (Gazzola et al., 2023). This Element adopts the latter view of LEP, as constantly shaped in a dynamic interaction of bottom-up and top-down forces. However prescriptive and regulatory policies might be in their inception, they are interpreted, shaped and altered by those acting out LEP (Johnson & Johnson, 2015). Stakeholders such as learners, parents and the public contribute to and co-construct policy daily (Spolsky, 2019). A nation-state passing policies on language education is a top-down, declared, deliberate, visible discourse of

LEP, created by politically dominant groups. A particular teacher debating with their class why they might want to study a language, or using their preferred teaching method, sits at the opposite end of the policy continuum. Enacted policy is largely invisible, but has great impact on LEP in practice, at the micro- and even meso-level. Both are embedded in their sociopolitical context, but their exposure to political ideology differs widely: at the macro-level, policy-making is subject to greater politicisation, by virtue of the combination of greater scrutiny, accountability and the need for ideological alignment with other, more general policy directives.

In this view of LEP, all actors involved in LEP are also engaged in formulating, debating and reshaping rationales for learning and creating (in)felicitous conditions for positive learner motivation. For these reasons, *discourses* on language learning are integral to LEP, not separate from it. Ideologisations of policies are expressed in texts describing and debating policies.

1.4 Policy–Practice Gaps in Language Education Policies

This section offers empirical underpinning for the argument that education systems, globally, experience Englishisation in the form of increased learning of English as a foreign language. It is not hard to find examples of LEP not reaching its targets due to English dominance, in both anglophone (Collen, 2020; Lanvers et al., 2021a) and non-anglophone (Wilkinson & Gabriëls, 2021a) contexts. To some extent, discrepancies between declared and practised LEP are inevitable: in the complex process of implementing LEP, intentions and rationales get interpreted, (mis)construed, diluted and distorted, as local agents of LEP apply their own resources, limitations, preferences, attitudes and ideologies (Johnson, 2013). Such discrepancies are most apparent when language education is obligatory: declared targets can be measured against actual uptake. Degrees of discrepancy are, however, also indicative of conflicts between different stakeholders involved in language learning: they reveal underlying tensions between those in power to declare LEP, and those enacting it (Johnson & Johnson, 2015).

1.4.1 Method and Structure

In this section, global language learning trends in formal school education are presented by region (anglophone/non-anglophone). Such a broad macro view necessitates a methodologically concise remit. In both anglophone and non-anglophone contexts, patterns are presented by large geographical areas. Official uptake figures of the last three decades on formal school foreign language (FL) uptake at upper secondary level are reported (where available), ordered by geographical area and, within this, largest data set available (e.g. the European

Union rather than their member states). For both anglophone and non-anglophone contexts, attitudinal and contextual challenges for LOTE learning are also discussed. The literature and data searches reveal, as so often in applied linguistics, a strong Global North bias in the literature and data available (Pennycook, 2020): precise data from many areas in the Global South remain less accessible than from the Global North.

1.4.2 Language Learning in Anglophone Contexts

1.4.2.1 Uptake Trends

Today, the term 'crisis' can be found frequently when describing language learning in many anglophone countries, such as the UK (Bowler, 2020), the US (Berman, 2011; Wiley, 2007) and Australia (Liddicoat & Scarino, 2010). As all major anglophone countries are now reporting language learning crises (Lanvers et al., 2021), trends suggest that we are facing the fulfilment of the prophecy – pronounced as early as 1996 – that English speakers will be the only monolinguals left (Skutnabb-Kangas, 1996). Across many anglophone contexts, compulsory schooling in LOTE has been eroded over the past decades (Lanvers, 2017a), and uptake of LOTE tends to lag behind official LEP targets.

In the UK, uptake of foreign language study has been reported as below target for over two decades now (British Academy, 2020; British Academy et al., 2020; British Council, 2017). In England, the government is currently on track to fail for a second time to meet its language education target for foreign language engagement, namely that 90 per cent should learn a foreign language up to the age of sixteen by 2025 (Lanvers, 2021). Scotland's national centre for languages reports a continual decline in uptake, of European languages especially, since 2012 (SCILT, n.d.). Recent policy changes to increase uptake at secondary level have as yet to make an effect on uptake (SCILT, n.d.). In Wales, the decline of FL uptake at the secondary level is more pronounced than in England (British Council, 2019). In Northern Ireland, uptake of FLs at age 14–16 has fallen by 19 per cent since 2010 (British Council, 2021). In Wales and Northern Ireland, Welsh and Irish respectively do not count towards a FL, partly explaining the low FL learning record in these nations. In Ireland, FLs were not compulsory at upper secondary level until very recently, and it is too early to determine if the new Languages Connect LEP will help stem the decline in FL uptake, especially of French, observed elsewhere (Bruen, 2021).

In the US, only about 20 per cent of school students leave with a FL certification (National K–12 Foreign Language Enrollment Survey Report, 2017), and only eleven states have a FL school graduation requirement. All FLs except for Spanish experienced a sharp decline over the last decades (Rhodes & Pufahl, 2014). Current language skills do not meet national requirements for trade, education, diplomacy and international cooperation (America's Languages, 2017; Rubio, 2018).

In Canada, official bilingual policies provide the context for high French–English bilingualism in some states, with an average of 20 per cent of Canadians reporting being bilingual in these languages. Despite governmental efforts, this percentage has not increased over the last decades, and English speakers are more likely to be monolingual than French speakers (Statistics Canada, 2023). Beyond this, Canada is one of the most linguistically diverse nations, with Mandarin and Punjabi as most common community languages (Statistics Canada, 2023) – to date, this multilingualism is not embedded in formal secondary school education.

In Australia, Asian languages, which make up the bulk of language learning at the upper secondary level, experienced a sharp decline over the last two decades (Baldwin, 2019), with uptake falling below target (Bunce, 2012). Foreign languages at any post-compulsory phase are in decline (Liddicoat & Scarino, 2010; Mason & Hajek, 2021). In New Zealand, the percentage of secondary school students aged 13+ enrolled in FL education dropped from 22.3 per cent in 2000 to 16.8 per cent in 2018 (East, 2021a), dropping as students advance through each school year, an attrition similar to that observed in England.

Across different anglophone contexts, there is a sharp social divide in the uptake of FLs. This divide is now documented in the UK (Lanvers, 2017b), the US (Cruickshank et al., 2020) and Australia (Molla et al., 2019). Learning languages other than English is often framed as a cultural asset for some privileged groups sharing the same cultural habitus, thus alienating large groups of learners not sharing this habitus (Coffey, 2018). Students in schools in disadvantaged areas may be prevented from continuing a LOTE against their own wishes (Brown 2019; Clayton, 2022). The decline in LOTE learning is often accompanied by a reduction in formal learning opportunities of FLs (America's Languages, 2017; BBC News, 2019). Many higher education providers struggle, for instance, to keep their languages departments viable (Liddicoat, 2022; Looney & Lusin 2019; Pawlak, 2022; Thompson, 2021).

1.4.2.2 Attitudinal Issues

Attitudes and beliefs in anglophone countries, such as the common mantra 'English is enough', are hard to break, even in the face of evidence to the contrary. Poor self-efficacy for FL learning is evidenced in many anglophone contexts (Lanvers, 2017a; Looney & Lusin, 2019). Negative public discourses, such as shaming learners for poor achievements, can further demotivate learners (Lanvers, 2017a), and attempts to motivate students better via fostering instrumental orientations alone tend to have little motivational effect on English L1 (first language) learners (Graham, 2022; Lanvers, 2017a).

Political changes unrelated to language can also impact negatively on language learning. In the UK, Brexit has jeopardised the aim to increase language learning, because Britain, having experienced a language teacher shortage for several decades, relies strongly on EU nationals as language teachers (Broady, 2020). Post-Brexit, these are both less willing and less able to settle in the UK. Negative commentary in journalistic outlets on the poor state of language learning in anglophone countries also deters students from FL study (Graham & Santos, 2015; Lanvers & Coleman, 2017) and thus widens the gap between societal needs for language skills, on the one hand, and actual language learning uptake, on the other (for the UK, see Foreman-Peck & Wang, 2014; for Ireland, see Schroedler, 2018).

Conversely, for the English speaker eager to engage in language learning, a number of hurdles are present (Lanvers, 2016a). Learners of English are keen to practise their target language with 'native speakers'. Thus, learners of LOTE who are fluent in English often find little opportunity to practise their target language. Furthermore, the demand to learn languages (via formal LEP) tends to be low in anglophone countries (Lanvers et al., 2021a). The predicaments of English L1 language learners remain poorly understood.

In such contexts, one might predict that anglophone language learners who *do* opt for language study beyond the compulsory phase are highly intrinsically motivated. This is indeed corroborated in empirical studies (for the UK: Lanvers, 2016b; Stolte, 2015; for the US: Thomson & Liu, 2018; for Australia: Lo Bianco & Slaughter, 2009). Even comparing learners of the same target language, for example English L1 and German L1 speakers both learning French, we observe that English L1 speakers show higher motivation than those with other L1s (Howard & Oakes, 2021).

1.4.3 Language Learning in Non-anglophone Contexts
1.4.3.1 Uptake Trends

In the following, I list some statistics and trends, underlining the (creeping) dominance in language learning in non-anglophone contexts. Across the European Union, language learners tend to perform better in English than in any LOTE they study, in terms of both uptake and learning outcomes (Lanvers et al., 2021b). Although formal engagement with the learning of LOTE is high at c. 60 per cent (Eurostats, 2022), learners and their parents often favour English as a foreign language, leading to a decline in the learning of French and other LOTE (Busse, 2017; Csizér & Lukács, 2010); across the European Union, targets for learning LOTE are not met (Lanvers, 2024).

In many low- and middle-income countries, English is needed to access education. The proficiency levels needed in English create a systemic barrier to access to education and academic success, and mother tongue teaching is sidelined by teaching via English or larger colonial languages (Kioko et al., 2014). Political will to increase teaching via students' L1, in line with UNESCO recommendations, is often present but progress in this respect is slow (for India, see Kanna & Rakesh, 2023; for further examples from South Africa, Australasia and Asia, see Menken & García, 2010). Regarding uptake of LOTE, the lack of publicly available data makes it hard to gauge general patterns in formal LOTE engagement at the upper secondary level across wide geographical regions, except for Europe and anglophone regions. However, at post-compulsory levels, global trends indicate that Asian languages (Mandarin, Japanese, Korean) are on the rise, while uptake of traditional FLs such as French, German and Italian is waning in both anglophone and non-anglophone contexts (for higher education generally, see Rose & Carson, 2014; for the US, see Looney & Lusin, 2019; for Asia, see Kobayashi, 2013).

One LEP aiming to reverse current trends is worthy of note. In China, the Chinese Ministry of Education launched a new LEP of investment and fostering of the learning of LOTE in 2016, in both upper secondary and tertiary education (Gao & Zheng, 2019). Notwithstanding the problems relating to the implementation of this policy and learning outcomes (Gao & Zheng, 2019), the policy nonetheless is a rare example of how modern language education policies explicitly aim to encourage the learning of LOTE. Currently, lack of public data on uptake and outcomes prevents a judgement on the long-term success of the policy.

1.4.3.2 Attitudinal Issues

Studies investigating motivation among dual linguistics (English and LOTE) in Europe tend to show higher motivation for English than LOTE (Henry, 2017; McEown et al., 2017), and, given the choice of learning English or LOTE, most would opt for English only (e.g. Dalmau, 2020; Dörnyei & Németh, 2006; Ushioda & Dörnyei, 2017). The preoccupation with English has been accompanied by a focus on pragmatic and instrumental rationales and motivations for language learning per se (Ushioda, 2017).

Studies in China reveal how learners see learning English as necessary but learning LOTE as a further opportunity to advance their career (e.g. Lu & Shen, 2022). As a good level of English competency is increasingly considered the norm, and necessary for academic progression, proficiency in English does not serve as well as a distinguishing marker of achievement. Thus, LOTE are becoming a 'good to also have' educational distinguisher (Lu & Shen, 2022), accompanied by a social divide in LOTE mirroring that in anglophone contexts, with learners from advantaged backgrounds more likely to develop fluency in a LOTE or two, in addition to English (e.g. in Spain, Codó & Sunyol, 2019; Rydenwald, 2015). Furthermore, negative emotions in LOTE learning can hamper progress among Chinese learners (Li & Liu, 2023).

There is, to date, no evidence that LOTE learning opportunities in non-anglophone contexts are declining during the *compulsory* phases of language learning. Researchers should, however, stay alert to the question of whether LEP and provision of LOTE learning in non-anglophone contexts might eventually follow the pattern observed in many anglophone contexts, namely that of policy deregulation and erosion of provision.

1.4.4 Summary: Language Learning Patterns

Languages other than English learning in both anglophone and non-anglophone contexts show some similarities across educational sectors and different geographical regions: a growing motivational crisis for the learning of LOTE, especially hitherto traditional LOTE such as European languages, and LEP-uptake mismatch. The uptake patterns in formal education underscore the notion that the phenomenal success of English as a global lingua franca has contributed to the spread of a monolingual mindset among anglophones (Ellis, 2008; Phillipson & Skutnabb-Kangas, 1996). The demise of learning opportunities for LOTE at school level has sharpened inequality in access to language learning (Barakos & Selleck, 2019). Anglophone contexts face a motivational crisis with respect to LOTE, a decline in uptake, increasing gaps between declared and practised policy and an erosion of the opportunities to study LOTE in their respective education systems. Elitist tendencies among those engaged in language learning can be observed across all major anglophone countries. Many academics have called for radical changes to the way anglophone countries approach language study (Broady, 2020; Copland & McPake, 2021; Reagan & Osborn, 2019). To a large extent, official policies do not match policy-in-practice at the level of schools, largely because learners may opt to study subjects other than languages ('voting with their feet').

Language Learning beyond English

Current gaps between declared and practised LEP support the thesis that, so long as LEP *permits* the displacement of LOTE by English, it will *serve* rather than *counter* English dominance – or 'linguistic imperialism', to use Phillipson's (1992) term. Concerning the EU's commitment to multilingual education, Phillipson (1992: 47) observes: 'although multilingualism seems to have become an "EU mantra", its actual extent falls far short of an equal treatment of the Union's official languages'. Citing the European Commission (2015) itself as evidence, he contends that the EU commitment to multilingualism has always been rhetorical rather than consequential. De Swaan is similarly critical of EU policy: 'in the Union, too, pious lip service is paid to the ideal of multilingualism, while, discreetly, only two languages are used in practice' (de Swaan 2002: 184). In his view, giving rights to medium-sized and smaller languages – often to redress English hegemony – can often have the opposite effect to the one intended: ' the more languages are formally assigned equal status, the less chance they stand of holding their own against the one dominant language, usually English, sometimes French' (de Swaan, 2002: 187).

While Phillipson attributes the failure of the European LEP to a lack of political commitment and the investment needed to fight linguistic imperialism, de Swaan ascribes the responsibility more to individuals who lack interest in diversifying their language learning. Both, however, agree that current European LEP permits English dominance to 'creep in' because no educational institution commands sufficient power (or willpower?) to stem English dominance. So long as the intentions of declared LEP diverge from key stakeholder interests (such as learners and educators), it is unlikely that LEP alone will be able to curb English dominance.

Unwittingly or not, the success of English as a global lingua franca has skewed existing views on rationales for language learning. To motivate learners of English, utilitarian and functional rationales and motivations are often foregrounded at the expense of holistic arguments (Graham, 2022). Learners of LOTE, meanwhile, face even greater motivational challenges (Ushioda & Dörnyei, 2017), leaving only the most determined LOTE learners with strong motivational stances persisting with their learning (Lanvers, 2016b). Both motivational problems relate to the success of Global English. In a novel departure, this Element conceptualises both motivational challenges in the context of Global English.

In a world 'stampeding towards English' (de Swaan, 2001a; van Parijs, 2020), how can we safeguard the learning of LOTE? What rationales might convince policymakers and curricula designers? Are the rationales we commonly cite suitable to motivate students? If attempts to engage learners in learning a variety of LOTE often fail to achieve their desired results, in both anglophone (Lanvers et al., 2021a) and non-anglophone (Busse, 2017) contexts, can Global English be blamed for this? In Germany, for instance, the teaching of French is in sharp decline, while the uptake of English continues to increase (Spiegel, 2023). It may seem self-evident to 'blame' Global English for any decline in LOTE learning. However, languages, including English, have no agency in themselves: language users do. Thus, the precise mechanisms leading to the 'stampede' towards English deserve more attention. Can we clearly identify which stakeholder groups are driving this 'stampede'? Learners? Parents? Policymakers? Conflicting interests between those preferring to learn English, or advocating LOTE, have long since reached the education sector. For instance, in German primary schools, it is customary, in border regions of neighbouring countries with different languages, to offer the neighbour's language and not English as first FL (e.g. Danish near the Danish border, French near the French border; see Lanvers, 2018a), a policy that has led parents to sue their local education authority for the right of their child to receive English instruction instead (Spiegel, 2007).

One explanation for the 'stampede' might be to point to a lack of motivation for the learning of LOTE on the part of the individual (learner or parent). This thesis conceptualises motivation for language learning as a 'fixed quantity': as motivation for one particular language increases, it decreases for others. Such framing contravenes modern conceptions of language learner motivation as dynamic, fluid and in constant ecological interaction with a host of internal as well as external influences (Gu, 2009). A further assumption underlying the 'individualistic' explanation concerns its overgeneralisation: the explanation takes as a given that most learners will be more motivated to learn language(s) of higher – as opposed to lesser – status. Section 4 discusses some learner groups that do not match this prediction.

One might also hold formal LEP accountable for the 'stampede' towards English and decline in LOTE learning. In this case, do LEPs merely follow (assumed) learner preferences, reinforcing the compulsory learning of English, while reducing the necessity to learn LOTE? This would portray LEP in the service of a neoliberal commodification of education (Bori & Canale, 2022).

In sum, blaming either individuals or LEP for the above-described trends has its limits, but both play a part: there is evidence that some learners are indeed motivated by personal advancement only when learning English (Bozzo, 2014), and that some LEP makers follow neoliberal principles in devising their LEP (Bori & Canale, 2022). Framing either LEP or learners themselves as responsible for the 'stampede' oversimplifies the complex interaction of policies, policy enactment at local and school level and learner motivation. In such

Language Learning beyond English 13

contexts, holistic rationales for language learning can serve as a bulwark against commodification of language study.

The next part of this section discusses the question of if English L1 speakers could be framed as 'advantaged' by not having to learn other languages.

1.5 English L1 Speakers as Beneficiaries of Global English

Some argue that L1 English speakers are unfairly advantaged, as they need not 'bother' with language learning (van Parijs, 2020), or that they are net gainers of the Global English phenomenon (Hultgren, 2020), because the English spoken in their inner circle (Kachru, 1992) is often perceived as a prestige and normative variety, desirable above other varieties. This section scrutinises these arguments.

Haberland (2020) and Wright (2009) remind us that English fluency does not guarantee mutual understanding: monolingual English speakers often lack sensitivity to the difficulties of using English as a lingua franca and may use colloquialisms, idioms, local sayings and regional accents that make conversation for a speaker using English as a lingua franca difficult (Jenkins, 2017). Such speakers may also make reference to UK- or US-specific cultural or political phenomena and acronyms, which leave the international interlocutor baffled (Hazel, 2016). Any purported advantage of having 'native speaker-like' competence (however defined) comes at a price: English L1 speakers struggle in international conversations using English as a lingua franca (Gilsdorf, 2002), partly because new and emerging forms of English are increasingly divergent from L1 speaker varieties, and partly because they have often had little opportunity themselves to practise cross-linguistic and cross-cultural communicative strategies that tend to develop alongside formal FL learning. Most importantly, however, since future varieties of English are increasingly being shaped by second-language speakers (Wei, 2020), any 'L1 English speaker advantage' in lingua franca communications seems doubtful.

Thus, it is timely to ask if English L1 speakers are indeed well served by being 'relieved of the burden' of language learning (van Parijs, 2020). Much like the cyclist 'relieved' of the cycle commute to work by opting for the bus, the indolence thereby gained – or freedom, depending on your perspective – comes at a price. Monolingualism is only increasing among L1 speakers of English (Lanvers et al., 2021; Skutnabb-Kangas, 1996), not in other language communities, and these monolinguals lose out on the social, cognitive and educational advantages that multilingualism brings with it (Bak, 2016). The 'English speaker advantage' reveals itself to be most valid if embracing a monolithic view of English (Pennycook, 2020), viewing English as a fixed entity with normative 'inner circle' standards (Kachru, 2006). Future varieties, however, including future high-status standards of English, will be determined by their users – and these are increasingly second- rather than L1 speakers.

The next section asks if current attitudes to the dominant lingua franca can also be found in the past.

1.6 Attitudes to Learning Lingua Francas: A Historical Outlook

Ostler (2005: 13) reminds us that world languages and lingua francas may come and go. The future of any lingua franca, however powerful it might seem at a particular historic moment, depends on a myriad of factors including demographic migration, access to language education and, increasingly importantly, communication technology. This brief historical excursus does not offer a like-for-like comparison between past lingua franca and Global English, nor does it offer any predictions regarding the future of Global English. Rather, it examines speakers' *attitudes* to historic lingua franca, including learning them.

As far as linguists are able to document, lingua francas, in the widest sense of a language used between groups who have no language in common (Berns, 2012), have existed for at least two millennia (Nolan, 2019), and multilingualism was a well-known phenomenon in antiquity (Schendl, 2012). The use of lingua francas has often benefited humankind, fostering the exchange of ideas, culture and science, as the use of Greek in early antiquity demonstrates. The Greek language was considered linguistically and culturally superior to any other (Adams, 2019), and Greeks generally did not feel the need to learn any languages other than their own (Momigliano, 1975). The term *barbarism* was coined and applied to any incomprehensible, foreign language, as well as to incompetent use of the Greek language (Hall, 1989).

With changing power dynamics within the Roman Empire, Greek culture and language became increasingly challenged (Adams, 2003), most vocally by Cicero (Fögen, 2000). Although ancient Greek continued to be of great importance for the educated elite for centuries to come (Leonhardt, 2013), speakers of Greek were increasingly compelled to add Latin to their repertoire (Dickey, 2015). Competence in Latin became a commodity for upwards social mobility, and desirable cultural and social capital (Adams, 2003).

This changed as the power dynamics of the Roman Empire shifted. The – to Romans, uncomfortable – asymmetry between Roman political and military prowess, and their nagging sense of cultural and linguistic inferiority vis-à-vis Greek (Adams, 2003), was increasingly challenged, most eminently by Cicero (Fögen, 2000). For those using Latin in antiquity, however, the notion of being *disadvantaged* by having to communicate in this second language (L2) was anathema. Like Greek, Latin continued to be learned and used long after the end of the Roman Empire, including in areas never occupied by the Romans (Leonhardt, 2013).

Both Latin and Greek survived as elite lingua francas for centuries, mainly thanks to meticulously guarded codification and, in teaching, adherence to a classical canon of texts, using traditional teaching methods. The codification of Latin is perhaps best illustrated by the sixteenth-century vogue for 'Ciceronianism', according to which only those words that were used by the classical author were deemed to be 'good enough Latin' to be used in teaching and writing (Leonhardt, 2013). Furthermore, in Europe, both French and Spanish gradually gained prestige from early modernity onwards (López, 2018), while the English language was at times described as 'passe Dover, [is] woorth nothing' (John Florio, 1578, cited in López, 2018: 55).

Through much of human history, then, multilingualism in prestige languages was a desirable asset for those holding privileged positions, with strongly codified prestige languages functioning as lingua francas, used alongside regional languages. In the seventeenth century, as nationhood became increasingly linked to linguistic identity, the powerful association between the nation-state and its language gave rise to the notion that monolingualism, rather than multilingualism, was an advantaged status. Indeed, according to Grambling (2016), this was the point when monolingualism was 'invented'. The notion served to sustain the hegemony of colonial powers and educated elites (Grambling, 2016). The following quotation by the seventeenth-century French essayist Dominique Bouhours expresses the sentiment of monolingual superiority succinctly:

> On parle déjà François dans toutes les Cours de l'Europe. Tous le étrangers qui ont de l'esprit, se piquent de sçavoir le François; ceux qui haïssent le plus nôtre nation, aiment nôtre langue; ... il n'y a guères de païs dans l'Europe où l'on n'entende le François, & il ne s'en faut rien que je ne vous avouë maintenant, que la connoissance des langues étrangers n'est pas beaucoup nécessaire à un François qui voyage. (Bouhours, 1671: 37–39)
>
> People are already speaking French in all the courts of Europe. All foreigners who have some intelligence are keen to know French, and those who most hate our nation, love our language ... there is hardly a country in Europe where one does not understand French, and there is no denying what I confess now, namely that the knowledge of foreign languages is not really needed by a travelling Frenchman.[1]

A simple substituting of the word *French* with *English* would suffice to update this quotation for the twenty-first century. Similar language-chauvinistic attitudes

---

[1] Translation by the author.

can be found in other contexts (e.g. García Bermejo, 2021). The exercise of comparing historical and current monolingual hegemonic attitudes may serve as a reminder – if it were needed – of the fragile status of any global language, when viewed longitudinally. This brief reflection on the status of past lingua francas, and attitudes towards language learning, has illustrated a number of characteristic dynamics that might apply to the current status of English, or not, as follows.

Being monolingual in a prestige lingua franca has historically been linked to a linguistic and cultural elite (Greek) or nation-state ideology. With changing political power dynamics, different language skills arise, a point at which monolinguals become disadvantaged. In today's context, this means that multilinguals rather than English monolinguals are better positioned to adjust to language shifts towards new prestige varieties, should the need arise. Furthermore, historically, learners of lingua francas tended to see language learning not as a burden, but rather as a privilege, permitting social betterment. Here, we observe a similarity to English today in that many learners of English are motivated by the professional and personal advantages this language might afford them (Lamb et al., 2019), while motivation for learning other languages declines (Busse, 2017). In short, for the minority of speakers of an elite lingua franca as (part of) their L1, learning other languages has previously been dismissed as superfluous, while opportunities to learn a lingua franca have always been framed positively.

However, mechanisms of diffusion, teaching and learning English differ substantially from learning past lingua francas. In today's English learning world, both elitism and standardisation, although not absent, are on the wane (Houghton & Hashimoto, 2018). Informal learning of English is greatly facilitated by the digital revolution, with boundaries between formal and informal learning, leisure and compulsory learning, institutional learning and self-study becoming ever more blurred (Socket, 2014). These key differences in learning opportunities and modes of learning provide something of an equaliser. Access to the learning of a global lingua franca has never had such a low entry point as access to English has today – even when acknowledging wide geopolitical differences in both accessibility to, and quality of, education. Access to free online resources is increasing (Shears, 2017); varieties and standards are becoming not only increasingly diverse but also increasingly unpredictable. This diversification precludes predictions as to if and when the language might lose mutual intelligibility, causing it potentially to break up into different languages (although such predictions exist; see Jenkins, 2017).

Furthermore, English currently benefits from neither unified codification (Leonhardt, 2013: 16) nor strong institutional control, such as what the Catholic church offered for Latin. Controversies around varieties and standards, including the native speaker debate, abound in the multibillion-dollar business that is TESOL (Teaching English to Speakers of Other Languages). Publications in journals such as *English Today, World Englishes*, and *TESOL Quarterly* illustrate this. Thus, while it is estimated that one third of the world's population will be involved in learning English in the near future (CEFR, 2020), there is no agreement on what counts as English. The dual impact of Covid-19 and the rise of online learning has made both the TESOL market and the English varieties taught more diverse, dynamic, fast changing and unregulated than ever (Gogolin et al., 2020).

In brief, the English L1 speaker could indeed be described as advantaged today in certain elite contexts, such as academic publishing – an advantage, however, that is subject to change the more English L2 speakers drop aspirations to adopt English L1 norms, and the more English is influenced by L2 speakers.

This historical excursus concludes with the observation that current *attitudes* towards learning and speaking a lingua franca do indeed find echoes in history. However, with respect to *dissemination* and *support mechanisms* for the lingua franca, significant differences have emerged. The lack of central control over codification and the mechanisms for learning and teaching English is unprecedented and serves as a warning to tread carefully when comparing the fate of past lingua francas to that of English. Current proliferation of varieties of English makes it hard to predict which variety of English – if any – learners might consider most worthwhile for investing in in the future. Lingua francas come and go, and at the present moment English is changing faster than other current lingua franca such as Spanish or Arabic (McWhorter, 2011). In an increasingly multilingual and globalised world, the one certainty about global language constellations and the forms taken by the lingua francas we have is that both will change, in status, form, and usage. Individuals and societies will need to adapt to these changes. In the current context, individuals versed in multilingual rather than monolingual practices will have the advantage of linguistic adaptability.

1.7 Terminologies

Perhaps more than other disciplines, the dynamic and fast-moving discipline of applied linguistics has its share of disputed terminology and definitions. From the 'native speaker' debate (Isaacs & Rose, 2021), to discussions about the term English versus *Englishes* (Rose & Galloway, 2017) or World Englishes, to the meaning of English as lingua franca (ELF) (Bolton, 2019), this Element inevitably touches upon linguistic conceptions and terminologies that have given rise to fundamental controversy. This section clarifies the terminology used here.

1.7.1 Anglophone and (Non-)Anglophone Contexts

Here, anglophone contexts are defined as those where the *majority of the population* grows up with English as (part of) their first language(s) *and* uses this language for both daily business and official communication, although all anglophone countries are de facto highly multilingual. In line with this definition, the EU, a pan-national entity where most of the population does not use English to conduct both daily and official business, will be classified as 'non-anglophone', while the US will be considered as anglophone. Likewise, for pragmatic reasons, anglophone *countries* are defined here as countries where most of the population grows up with English as (part of) their first language(s).

1.7.2 Englishisation, Englishising

These terms are used to denote the phenomenon whereby English is used in contexts *where hitherto other languages were used*. Thus, it can cover a wide range of linguistic phenomena, such as:

- an increase in the use of English loan words and all forms of translanguaging involving English
- the move towards using English as a medium of instruction
- in LEP, greater emphasis on the development of English rather than LOTE
- in education institutions, curriculum and staffing changes favouring knowledge of language, linguistics and culture associated with English

1.7.3 Motivation in Language Learning

It has often been argued that motivation for learning languages is somewhat unique compared to learning other subjects (Ushioda, 2012) in that language learning offers the potential for widening social horizons, for access to different cultures and for developing new facets of identity. This complexity is undoubtedly one of the reasons for the plethora of theoretical approaches and empirical works on the topic (for meta reviews, see e.g. Aryadoust, 2023; Mahmoodi & Yousefi, 2022), which makes it all the more important to clarify the understanding of language learner motivation for the purpose of this Element. Space precludes a full discussion of the relative merits of currently dominant L2 motivation theories (for a discussion, see e.g. Lamb et al., 2019), but two features common to the dominant theories currently used in research stand out: a basic extrinsic–intrinsic continuum dimension, and a psychosocial dimension. In other words: all L2 learning motivation theories agree that (1) individual learners personally identify with reasons for language study to very different extents, and (2) the social environment, 'significant others' and the wider sociocultural environment influence learners greatly. These minimal premises for L2 motivation, supported by the current L2 motivation literature, serve as the basis for conceptualising L2 in this Element and for recommending pedagogical practices to promote learner motivation (Section 4). As a result, although one motivational theory is preferred over others (self determination theory), the pedagogical recommendations in this Element are designed to be compatible with all currently dominant L2 motivation theories.

1.7.4 Languages Other than English (LOTE)

Despite its intended neutrality, LOTE is inadequate in its anglocentricity, juxtaposing some 7,000+ existing languages in the world against one language, which, moreover, is not even the first or second most spoken language as L1 in the world (Ethnologue, 2019). Despite criticism of the term (Cunningham, 2019), there is no agreement on alternative(s) to it. Introducing alternative terminology is possible, of course, but at the expense of comprehensibility and accessibility. Loathed or liked, the term LOTE is now established, and alternative nomenclature is unlikely to successfully replace existing terms. The use of alternative terminology risks marginalising and fragmenting academic discourse. Moreover, it is appropriate in this context in that learning of English and LOTE are explicitly contrasted. Thus, the term LOTE is used here in the tradition of linguistic *reclaiming* from negative connotations, such as in feminist linguistics (Godrej, 2011).

1.7.5 L1, L2, LX, FL, Learners of English, Learners of LOTE

The debates on how to label the language competencies of individuals, in particular the language acquired as an infant, are well into their third decade (Cook, 1999) and show little sign of abating. Avoiding the term 'native speaker' for all its infelicitous connotations (Isaacs & Rose, 2021), the question nonetheless arises of how to refer to the language competencies an individual develops via informal exposure in infancy, as opposed to any other languages learned subsequently, whether informally or formally. A common practice in linguistics is to use numerical ordering to indicate the chronology of acquisition: L1 versus L2, L3 and so on, in an attempt to eschew value judgements about an individual's proficiencies in any specific language. This practice is adopted in all contexts *where an order of language learning* can be assumed, based on context and LEP. In Germany, for instance, requirements of language learning are often expressed as 'first foreign language to be introduced', 'second foreign language to be introduced' and so forth, often leaving some freedom as to which target languages these should be. The label 'L1' is open to criticism similar to that of 'native speaker', with respect to connotations of proficiency and order of acquisition. It is an inadequate descriptor of multilingual L1 acquisition, interrupted and fragmented L1 acquisition, and so on, as often experienced by children, for instance those raised in migrating families. The canonical ordering poses a similar problem for further languages, in that it falsely connotes a neat chronology in which languages were/are learned. Dewaele (2018) proposes the terms L1 and LX, the former describing a first language, *usually* mastered at a high level of competency, and the latter for any subsequently learned language, to avoid such misrepresentations. This practice is adopted here, with some important demarcations: the term 'L1' is understood as *any language(s) a given speaker is first exposed to and acquires as an infant*. Thus, 'English L1', for instance, is to be read as shorthand for any speaker who has this language either as the sole or one of their first languages. Furthermore, 'LX' will be used to describe any language learned *via formal schooling*, reflecting the Element's focus on LEP in the school sector. The LX will only be afforded a specific number (L3, L4 etc.) if the order is clearly identifiable via LEP, as for example in German LEP. The term *foreign language* (FL) is used here to describe any language(s) acquired via formal schooling. Finally, the terms 'learners of English' and 'learners of LOTE' are not to be understood as mutually exclusive. Indeed, Section 4 dedicates a section to the problem of motivation in learners simultaneously acquiring English and LOTE.

1.7.6 Polity

Kaplan and Baldauf (1997) stipulate that LEP needs to be captured at the level of polity, that is, the entity that is responsible for LEP and existing practices and preferences. Language education policymakers thus have agency in language learning, in the sense of deciding who may, or need to, learn what language to what level, and how to justify these policies as part of a complex ecological mesh of sociocultural and political factors.

1.7.7 Plurilingualism and Multilingualism

This Element adopts the Common European Framework of Reference (CEFR, 2020) definition of plurilingualism: the ability on the part of the *individual* to use several languages. Conversely, multilingualism is used to describe this ability for a *geographical area*, that is, the handling of more than two languages by some or all members of a *society* (Aronin, 2006: 3). Both terms are used according to CEFR definitions here.

Both the multilingual and translanguaging turns in applied linguistics foreground the *plurilingual* learner identity in any language learning processes.

Language Learning beyond English 21

These paradigm shifts mandate for all language knowledge to be validated equally in learning contexts. Section 2 expands further on how we might assist educators and learners towards a positive validation of all language skills, using the recent framework of *dynamic language constellations*.

1.7.8 Rationale for Language Learning

One of the curiosities of the LEP literature is that the term *rationale* is often used but seldom defined. Here, *rationale* is used in the dictionary sense (Encyclopedia Britannica, n.d.) of *logical reasons*; thus, LEP rationales serve to legitimise and justify policies using rational arguments.

1.7.9 World Englishes, Lingua Franca, Global English, World Language

Given the plethora of publications and ever-expanding terminologies describing growth in the use and learning of English, a pragmatic restriction to commonly used terminology, in its most widely accepted definition, is called for. A *lingua franca* is understood as a variety used for communication between speakers of different L1s (Leonhardt, 2013). The term *world language* is used here to refer to a language of high global status, often used in high-status domains, such as politics, business and commerce, travel, high culture, and academia. The term *World Englishes* describes varieties of English used around the globe, giving no preference or partiality towards one variety or another (Seargeant, 2010). Finally, the term *Global English* is used here, again following Seargeant's (2010) taxonomy, to underline the use of English beyond the inner circle countries and in global professional contexts, in the widest sense. In other words, Global English is a phenomenon *powered by* Englishisation, in all its forms, including the learning of English where, conceivably, none had taken place previously.

1.8 Section Summary

In a context where one language, by virtue of its global status, has the power to influence the LEP of all other languages, it is timely to consider what rationales for language learning might offer solutions to the challenge of English dominance. The historical excursus served to underline the ephemeral nature of lingua franca, and the advantages of preparedness for global linguistic changes. This section also outlined commonalities between anglophones and non-anglophones regarding the effect of Global English: as the learning of English is prioritised over that of learning LOTE – by learners themselves and/or by LEPs. There are also signs that the learning of LOTE is becoming increasingly elite, especially in anglophone and increasingly in non-anglophone contexts. In anglophone contexts, neither the 'English is enough' fallacy (Martin, 2010) nor elitism in LOTE learning (Muradás-Taylor, 2023) show signs of fading. These trends seem to support de Swaan's (2001b) thesis that learners are mostly interested in learning high-status languages. Meanwhile, multilinguality, including in language classrooms, is growing globally, often due to mass migration. As a result, education systems and formal language education are increasingly diverging from the lived realities of multilingualism today (Lo Bianco & Aronin, 2020: 40).

A rethinking of rationales for language study can help address this gap. Helping learners appreciate a wide range of reasons for language study is as important as language instruction itself and can help learners appreciate the value of learning a variety of languages. Thus, rationales can do more than offer a (necessary) justification for the space accorded to languages in the curriculum and learners' overcrowded timetables. The question *Why teach or learn languages?* supersedes operational questions such as *How? At what age?* and *To what level?* These can only be addressed meaningfully once the first is answered. Too often, however, neoliberal approaches to education drive language education policymakers to address questions of *how* before *why*.

A crucial consideration in rationalising language learning for the twenty-first century is if English can somehow be 'blamed' for current language learning uptake trends. The next section offers a critical debate on this issue.

2 Framing English as a Killer Language

> It happens all too often – people regret that their language and culture are being lost but at the same time decide not to saddle their own children with the chore of preserving them. (Dalby, 2020: 252)

Section 1 has argued that, globally, provision and uptake of formal language education are at a crossroads, in several respects: declared aims in LEP are not matched by actual uptake, and neither declared LEP nor uptake match the reality of our increasingly diverse and multilingual world (Banks et al., 2016). This section scrutinises the link between Global English and LOTE learning in more detail. As a first step towards unpacking any assumed link between patterns in the learning of LOTE and of English, the next section engages with the question of whether Global English can be framed as responsible for the decline in LOTE learning.

2.1 Relating Global English to the Decline in LOTE Learning

The answer to the question of whether Global English is responsible for a decline in LOTE learning depends to a large extent on the degree of partisanship or neutrality afforded to the English language, as both a lingua franca and a favourite FL for learners. The positioning of English (e.g. as a commodity, a threat, a neutral affordance) influences stakeholders' view of the relative merit of learning English and shapes LEP. Declared LEPs might favour English explicitly, for example by increasing the compulsory element of English L2 in the curriculum or, implicitly or even inadvertently, by liberalising choices in the learning of L2s (Phillipson, 2017b).

Similarly, the stance someone takes towards the phenomenon of Global English shapes how they explain the language learning crises in anglophone contexts. For some, the crisis is taken as evidence of xenophobia, native-speakerism and a chauvinistic and imperialistic stance towards English. This explanation, plausible at first glance, becomes problematic when looking more closely at who 'decides' to learn languages – or not. Who has elected to deprioritise language learning in anglophone education systems? Do learners actively 'decide' not to learn a LOTE and, if so, why? In the UK's education systems, for instance, a range of systemic disincentives prevent students from continuing with FL study beyond the compulsory phase (Lanvers, 2018b), with some forced to discontinue their study (Clayton, 2022). Thus, the 'choice' to study a FL is often conditioned by forces outside the remit of the students themselves. There are also few signs that English L1 speakers harbour more chauvinistic attitudes towards their first language than any other L1 speakers might do towards theirs: all speakers show the tendency to prefer their own language (Garret, 2010). In sum, there is little evidence to support the claim of 'English exceptionalism', in the sense that English L1 speakers are more averse to language learning per se than other L1 speakers.

There is, however, evidence that, like other L1 speakers, English L1 speakers often show a preference for their native variety, rather than a variety emerging out of ELF use (Subtirelu & Lindemann, 2016), a fact that often contributes to miscommunication between L1 and L2 users of English (Hazel, 2016). As argued in Section 1, monolingualism tends to equip L1 English speakers poorly for ELF communication. To date, the few empirical studies investigating the issue suggest that many anglophones are aware of these communicative limitations (Cruickshank et al., 2020; Lanvers, 2012).

In sum, both the notion of English L1 speaker 'advantage' and the notion of English as the killer language of LOTE need revisiting. To scrutinise both notions further, three models of global language constellations will be presented. Many such models exist (e.g. Kachru, 2006). The three models presented here have been chosen for heuristic purposes: the models offer maximally contrastive answers to the questions of whether, and how, Global English might be bringing changes to the learning of English, on the one hand, and of LOTE, on the other. They are:

- Linguistic imperialism
- Global language system
- Dominant language constellations

The models frame Global English, respectively, as inherently hegemonic, inherently utilitarian or as part of a dynamic unitary system. Each model is examined from the perspective of the *language learner*: learners of English and learners of LOTE (including English L1 learners), asking how these learners are positioned within these models in the context of Global English; are they beneficiaries or losers? Thus, this section discussed the level of agency the different models might ascribe to language learners themselves.

2.2 Linguistic Imperialism

For some linguists (Pennycook, 1994; Phillipson, 2003), English has long ceased to be, and never will be, a neutral lingua franca. In Phillipson's view, standards of English, access to language learning and status hierarchies of different Englishes remain intrinsically linked to, and representative of, socio- and geopolitical inequalities. While others (e.g. Hultgren, 2020) consider today's ubiquity of English as a sign of the language's equalising potential, if not its de facto equalising quality, Phillipson (1992: 47) sees English dominance as safeguarded by the 'establishment and continuous reconstruction of structural and cultural inequalities between English and other languages'. Any form of linguistic imperialism is viewed as a form of *linguicism*, defined as 'ideologies, structures and practices which are used to legitimate, effectuate, regulate and reproduce an unequal division of power and resources (both material and immaterial) between groups which are defined on the basis of language (Phillipson & Skutnabb-Kangas, 1996: 667).

Phillipson (2003) asserts that linguicism perpetuates and reinforces existing social inequality. In this view, discourses that frame English as neutral (*lingua nullius* – nobody's language), as espoused by the British Council or some American politicians, contribute to linguicism and mask the vested interests of dominant powers in its proliferation.

2.2.1 Critique of Linguistic Imperialism

As detailed theoretical critiques are available elsewhere (Lin, 2013), this review concentrates on how *stakeholders* in language education are positioned within the linguistic imperialism model. De Swaan has criticised its strong hegemonic view of English, arguing:

> Recently, a movement to right the wrongs of language hegemony has spread across the Western world, advocating the right of all people to speak the language of their choice, to fight 'language imperialism' abroad and 'linguicism' at home, to strengthen 'language rights' in international law. Alas, what decides is not the right of human beings to speak whatever language they wish, but the freedom of everyone else to ignore what they say in the language of their choice. (De Swaan 2001a: 52)

In other words, however ideologically driven some declared policy may or may not be, practised policy can never be organised in the controlled manner that Phillipson postulates. Gaps between declared and practised policy are inevitable, and, in the continual tension between top-down policy and bottom-up practice, the agency of individuals must be acknowledged. Learners might *choose* English, for their own betterment and that of their communities. Indeed, the most vocal criticism of Phillipson can be found among those advocates of English who highlight the liberational, life-enhancing and mobility-enhancing potential afforded by the language (Canagarajah, 1999). Many of Phillipson's opponents share his critical assessment of English dominance, but differ greatly in their approaches to addressing it.

Phillipson (2013), aware of such criticism, has argued that neither individuals, nor LEPs, nor the applied linguistics academic community have so far succeeded in countering linguistic imperialism. For him, inequalities in access to learning English and the continuing higher status of inner circle (Kachru, 2006) varieties of English are mechanisms that perpetuate linguistic imperialism.

In sum, advocates of the linguistic imperialism model tend to contend that the language is 'imposed' upon learners against their will and thereby afford little agency to the individual learner as agents of LEP. The position reveals a conceptualisation of LEP as static. As Canagarajah (1999) remarks, Phillipson emphasises the structural at the expense of the local. If, however, we credit language users with agency to shape, propagate and form their own varieties and norms, even the learning of a language labelled 'imperialistic' harbours the potential for resistance. Learners may take ownership of varieties of English, distribution processes and resources in English. Free online learning resources, increasingly ubiquitous, facilitate such bottom-up processes, and learners need not replicate and reinforce dominant varieties of English (Seidelhofer, 2005). In short, language learners and users have agency.

2.3 Global Language System

The economic linguists De Swaan (2002), Grin (2008) and Calvet (2006) have proposed a hierarchical global language system. In this system, only about 100 of the world's several thousand languages are positioned as *central*; these are spoken by 95 per cent of the global population. Furthermore, some twelve languages (e.g. Russian, German, French, Arabic, Hindi, Spanish) achieve the status of *supercentrality*, reaching significance beyond national boundaries, and only one language, English, achieves *hypercentral* status, as a global lingua franca. Viewing language as a hyper-collective economic good, the model furthermore states that language learning mostly occurs in a centripetal direction, with most learners interested in learning languages of higher centrality than the ones they already possess as (part of) their first language(s). As a consequence, the only hypercentral language becomes the most desirable to learn. The model is a perfect example of self-reinforcement of hierarchies: any existing popularity is likely to propel a language into further popularity, and vice versa (de Swaan, 2002: 5).

The model includes a mechanism for calculating the economic status of a given language in the form of its *Q value* (de Swaan, 1993). To do so, the overall number of speakers of a language and the number of multilinguals among them are needed: the Q value of any language is calculated by multiplying the *prevalence* of a language (number of speakers) by its *centrality* (number of multilingual speakers). It thus would be in the language learner's interest to invest time and effort into languages with a high Q value. If individuals have a choice between a higher- or lower-status language (as measured by Q value), for instance when an author needs to decide which language to publish in, economic and expediency arguments usually favour the higher-status language, while ethical and cultural arguments, such as countering hegemony and preserving diversity in cultures, might favour a lower-status language. In multilingual societies and communication systems, centrality rather than prevalence of a language will dictate which language carries a higher Q value and is likely to function as the more expedient lingua franca. Furthermore, *linguistic inertia* (de Swaan, 2002: 18) is often responsible for a time lag between changes in political constellations and shifts in the status of various languages, including the popularity of learning a specific language, but, in many cases, power dynamics between languages ultimately align with those of the political world. The model

Language Learning beyond English 27

thus predicts a continual dynamic rivalry between languages, each vying to improve its position:

> The concept of a multi-tiered, hierarchical world language system provides the foundations for a political sociology of language. The dynamics of this emerging global system were generated by processes of state-formation, which led to language unification at home, and to transcontinental expansion of the language abroad. Within each constellation, group rivalry and accommodation, and elite attempts at closure, shape the division of functions between languages. (de Swaan 2002: 52)

Meanwhile, L1 speakers of a high-status language such as English are framed as 'relieved' of the burden of language learning, often without much awareness of this privilege ('an enviable blessing is bestowed upon them by the sheer accident of their mother tongue', de Swaan 1998: 43).

As for the issue of linguistic imperialism, de Swaan positions this rather more ethical question outside the remit of linguistics, and counters, similarly to Canagarajah, that most choices for or against a given language are determined bottom-up, by speakers themselves. For de Swaan, then, language preferences of individuals should not be subject to ethical considerations of linguistic human rights, and top-down LEPs, for the most part, try to address the preferences of most learners at most times.

2.3.1 Critique of de Swaan

In this model, competitiveness, profitability and efficiency determine global language developments, including learning trends (Del Percio & Flubacher, 2017). The desirability of a language is as calculable as the price of goods. Phillipson (2003) observes that de Swaan borrows from neoliberal theories of international trade, of merit goods and collective cultural capital. In de Swaan's model, learners are first and foremost agents improving their linguistic capital by acquiring high Q-value languages. The dynamics of language distribution, then, would be akin to the mechanisms that characterise social media postings, namely user-driven, bottom-up and populist, thus mostly reinforcing existing hierarchical linguistic structures. Language education policymakers, meanwhile, would be largely guided by the Q values of both L1s and L2s in play in any given context, and macro-political, economic and social factors would determine which L2s (if any) were worthwhile learning. In this model, the main task of declared LEP is to strategically align provision with individual preferences, matching maximum opportunities for individuals to develop their Q value in return for minimal investment.

This model suffers from the opposite to the imperialist, emphasising the local at the cost of the structural, to paraphrase Canagarajah. It frames individuals as those acting out language choices as if (relatively) free from the forces of declared LEP. However, in formal compulsory language education, many learners have little choice over when to learn which language, for how long and how well. However, learning opportunities are determined by education policies, in turn shaped by sociopolitical priorities – set by forces well outside the control of the individual learner. Furthermore, language is more than an economic good, and both learner motivation and official rationales for language teaching go beyond the utilitarian.

In sum, Phillipson conceptualises English hegemony as generated systemically, De Swaan as organically generated. Both, however, focus on utilitarian benefits of language skills. One consequence of this bias is that, in both models, English L1 speakers may be framed as 'privileged'. As argued in Section 1, this needs increasingly to be queried, not only because English L1 speakers remain ill equipped for international communication but also because their opportunities to learn LOTE are diminishing. The next section presents a global languages model that frames *all* language skills as working cumulatively and enriching the learner's linguistic repertoire in more than a utilitarian sense: dominant language constellations (DLC).

2.4 Dominant Language Constellations

Aronin (2006) first proposed the concept of DLC to refer to a 'person's most expedient languages, functioning as an entire unit and enabling an individual to meet all his/her needs in a multilingual environment' (Aronin, 2019: 21). Dominant language constellations accentuate speakers' fluctuating rather than static language use. How, then, do individual DLC relate to global language constellations? The interdependence between an individual and their multilingual environment shapes individual DLC, which in term shapes those at the meso and macro levels. Societal and individual language changes emerge as a result of a dynamic interplay at the micro, meso and macro level. For instance, the twenty-first century global rise in multilingualism (Aronin & Singleton, 2008) can be partly explained by globalisation but also by increasing diversity and complexity in personal lives. Aronin (2019) observes that in Europe as elsewhere, most immigrants are trilingual, speaking their L1, their community language and English. A key difference to the two models discussed earlier is that languages are not conceptualised as static, monolithic and separate. Instead, a plurilithic view of languages, conceptualising each language without fixed boundaries, allows us to see that not only do all language competencies cumulatively form an individual's language repertoire but also all competencies interact in a multidirectional manner. Recent insights into cross-linguistic

Language Learning beyond English 29

interaction in language learning from cognitive linguistics either support the thesis of one common underlying proficiency across all language competencies (Cummins, 2021) or go so far as to propose a fully unitary cognitive system across all languages (Wei, 2018).

Meanwhile, in LEP and educational practice, monolithic paradigms of languages, at times accompanied by nation-state ideologies, still dominate (Lo Bianco & Aronin, 2020). Bilingual education programmes, if present at all, are often conceptualised with reference to historical rather than contemporary bilingualism, offering few concessions to the cultural and linguistic diversities found in modern classrooms. Dominant language constellations, by contrast, adopt a plurilithic paradigm of language use and learning: in any plurilingual, no language system operates independently from others. As a result, multilingualism is not framed as a potential threat to social cohesion, nor is multilingual education necessarily seen as the most important tool to increase social cohesion (Newby et al., 2009).

In DLC, the dynamics of the language constellation follow the principles of dynamics systems theory: the interaction of different languages and different language constellations is in constant flux, at the micro, meso and macro levels. In this complex interaction of many individual and societal DLC, different languages may take marginalised or central positions at different times and in different places, influenced by both internal and external factors (Lo Bianco & Arorin, 2020). No *one* DLC, however multilingual, would offer an optimal stable solution for all communication contexts. Rapidly changing multilingual practices are well evidenced in the communications of users of English as a lingua franca (House, 2011), who use their *entire* language repertoire effectively to communicate.

In sum, the DLC model conceptualises all language skills as assets, and none as a threat, while acknowledging that monolingualism limits one's language repertoires. Currently, and not always by choice, English L1 speakers in English lingua franca communications often have the poorest language repertoire (Lanvers et al., 2021).

The preceding models of language systems give different answers to the question as to whether L1 speakers of English are advantaged. The global language system (de Swaan) and linguistic imperialism (Phillipson) models position anglophones as net gainers of the Global English phenomenon (Hultgren, 2020), for two reasons: on the one hand, their inner circle (Kachru, 1992, 2006) varieties of English tend to be perceived as more prestigious, desirable and normative, and, on the other, anglophones are framed as being relieved of the 'burden of language learning' (van Parijs, 2020). In light of the fact that English is also shaped by L2, not L1 speakers (Wei, 2020), and of the increasing evidence of the social, cognitive and educational advantages of multilingualism (Bak, 2016), both claims need to be re-examined.

Unlike the two other models, DLC offers a more nuanced answer to the question *Are English L1 speakers advantaged?* The answer depends on the circumstances of the speakers: are they sensitive to the needs of those using English as a lingua franca? Do they have opportunities to learn and practise other languages, and, if so, is LOTE learning facilitated? Dominant language constellations have an equally nuanced reply to the question of whether language constellations are mostly shaped by top-down or bottom-up forces. DLC sees *both* declared and practised policy as arising in the intersection of broader sociopolitical and local, regional and personal interests. Language education policy, whether of the official, declared kind or the practised kind, is a locus not only where vested interests in languages manifest themselves but also, equally, where change (for better or worse) can be enacted. Socially responsible LEP, then, should embrace these opportunities and add social and educational justice to its concerns about linguistic justice (Jenkins, 2020). Research agendas for DLC linguists interested in language education include the following: *Is access to language education fair and equitable? Does LEP address existing linguistic inequalities? Does LEP address the linguistic needs of the (plurilingual) learner and the multilingual society they live in? How does LEP ensure equitable distribution of language education resources?* The emphasis on social engagement and responsibility positions the DLC linguist at the intersection of research agendas in applied linguistics and education: social justice in education and linguistic justice. This Element consequently adopts DLC as the framework for studying global language constellations, and language learning within these.

2.5 Section Summary

This section debated if Global English can be described as a 'killer' of LOTE learning. At first glance, global patterns of language learning, described in Section 1, seem to support this thesis, as do some conceptualisations of global language systems. Although Phillipson and De Swaan differ greatly as to the relative merit of Global English, the authors' utilitarian models of language broadly align with materialist and instrumental rationales of language learning: either the system of linguistic hegemony compels the learner to focus on some language(s) at the expense of others (Phillipson), or the Q value seduces the learner to do the same (De Swaan). In both models, the aim of maintaining diversity and equity in language learning would thus be an uphill struggle. Overtly utilitarian conceptualisations of language, and of rationales for language learning, do indeed open the door to the English as a 'killer language' argument. Such narrow rationales are often propagated within educational systems themselves, leaving both learners and educators vulnerable to accepting and reproducing them (Lanvers & Graham, 2022).

Moving away from a purely utilitarian understanding of language learning, DLC offers a different solution. Conceptualising all language knowledge as a repertoire, whereby learning any language is an opportunity to enrich one's overall linguistic repertoire, languages act not in competition but in cooperation. To date, however, most language policies generally, and LEP especially, are still a long way from adopting such paradigms.

The next section discusses rationales for language learning and asks *How can we best justify language learning in the age of Global English?* The first subsection revisits a range of commonly cited rationales for language learning, asking how they might stand up to the Global English challenge. The section then presents a new matrix of rationales for language learning, which aligns with the plurilithic paradigm derived from DLC and conceptualises such rationales not as oppositional but rather as complementary to one another.

3 Rationales for Language Learning: A Twenty-First Century Matrix

3.1 Introduction

Historically, the main purpose of rationales for language study has been to justify the place of FL in the curriculum. Legitimising language education (and thus justifying public investment) in any education system is bound by the fundamental functions of all education:

(1) to create human capital for the nation's economy,
(2) to promote equality and cohesion,
(3) provide citizens with a sense of identity (Byram, 2008a).

All three legitimisations have implications for LEP, curricula design and language pedagogy. By formulating justifications for language learning, a political entity also formulates a position on the collective identity they aspire to, and their national and international outlook. In other words, the significance of rationales in the development of LEP and curricula cannot be overstated.

Academics have asked that 'rationales for studying languages should be collected and classified' (Kelly & Jones, 2003: 35) to guide policymakers and pedagogues in their language policy planning. Hitherto, classifications of rationales tended to be presented listwise, or following a dichotomous classification, for instance of enrichment versus functional rationales (Hawkins, 2005;

Mitchell, 2003). This Element answers the call for a 'classification of rationales' with the intention to serve not only policymakers and pedagogues but also learners themselves. The matrix of interconnected rationales presented here not only does better justice to the *interdependence* of rationales but also offers a robust *foundation to motivate learners* holistically for language study, and thus provides an answer to the challenges of language learning in the shadow of a (currently) dominant lingua franca.

The section is structured as follows: Section 3.2 gives a brief overview of rationales for language learning to date. It concludes by calling for a holistic conceptualisation of rationales for language study. Section 3.3 proposes a dynamic matrix of rationales, conceptualised according to two questions: *Who benefits from language learning?* and *What is the nature of the benefit?* The matrix proposes two continuum dimensions: on the level of *beneficiary* of L2 learning, a dimension ranging from the individual to society, and on the level of *nature of benefit*, a continuum ranging from material to non-material benefits. Section 3.4, then, in a novel departure, discusses how rationales might link to learner motivation. For this purpose, a widely used learner motivation theory, which has already been brought to bear on language learning research, *self determination theory* (SDT), serves to provide a theoretical underpinning.

3.2 Rationales for Language Learning to Date

Historically, most *formal* language learning, a prerogative of the elite, tended to serve a wide range of cultural and humanistic purposes, rather than provide any utilitarian benefit. The beginning of the twentieth century saw the emergence of a broad distinction between utilitarian and educational purposes for language study (Hawkins, 2005), with educational rationales subsuming a range of arguments under one umbrella, sometimes labelled 'intrinsic', 'cultural' or 'enrichment'. The basic utilitarian–educational distinction was often accompanied by the tacit assumption that enrichment purposes were somewhat more laudable, and also more achievable within educational contexts, in contrast to instrumental and vocational arguments. On the one hand, pedagogues might query if educational systems are sufficiently equipped to deliver language skills of the standards needed for professional practical purposes (Hawkins, 2005), or if such practical purposes of L2 study are sufficiently significant to warrant any comprehensive teaching at school level. On the other hand, academics especially have tended to view utilitarian rationales with some scepticism (Hawkins, 2005), fearing this would truncate the wider merits of language study.

The utilitarian/non-utilitarian polarisation of rationales has furnished a breeding ground for debates regarding the educational value of L2 learning.

Language Learning beyond English   33

The early 2000s saw this debate intensified, especially in the UK and the US: a time of significant political and educational change in both contexts. There was an increased urgency to address the looming question of the purposes of LOTE study in the context of Global English, and the position any LOTE might have in the curriculum.

Utilitarian rationales were used, in the main, to justify formal and compulsory language learning (Mitchell, 2003). Notwithstanding this, within educational contexts, many attempts to encourage amotivated and directionless students rely on instrumental and material arguments, along with educational incentivisation (Lanvers, 2017a; 2018b). However, recent evidence, especially coming from language learners with English L1, suggests that such arguments alone tend to achieve little in terms of changing learner attitude and motivation (Lanvers & Graham, 2022; Ushioda, 2017). Such arguments may even be counterproductive: by encouraging learners to develop a utilitarian understanding of the purpose of language study, students may counter that 'English is enough' after all, and struggle to develop different and more holistic orientations (Coffey, 2018; Lanvers, 2017b).

The twenty-first century has brought new evidence on the benefits of language learning (Kramsch, 2005, 2014). Educators are resorting to a more comprehensive range of answers regarding the purpose and benefits of studying *any* language (Gallagher-Brett, 2004), including many arguments that do not necessarily favour the study of any particular language, and are thus applicable to a wide range of LOTE. The challenge for conceptualising rationales for language learning in the twenty-first century, then, lies not so much in defending LOTE learning per se, but in responding to the challenging language learning context created by Global English. Currently, a common answer to this challenge is to associate the dominant lingua franca learning with utilitarian rationales, and LOTE with 'other' rationales – an unhelpful association that the matrix presented in this section aims to correct. The next section offers a brief historic overview of language learning rationales, with a special focus on rationales in the context of Global English.

Mitchell (2003: 9f) was among the first to differentiate more finely between different enrichment-type rationales (*language as intellectual discipline, as vehicle of high culture, as means for personal self-development, for exploring alternative cultures*), designed to broaden our understanding of those purposes hitherto labelled 'educational'. Nonetheless, in the UK, debates on LEP during the early 2000s remained shaped by the binary thinking of instrumental/vocational versus educational rationales. Politically, this debate marked a controversial move by the English government, in 2004, to make language study optional beyond age fourteen in England. Some argued that poor learning outcomes overall do not provide a sufficiently strong base for language teaching for any utilitarian purposes, and compulsory language education should therefore be discontinued (Williams, 2001). Others argued that vocational orientations narrow learners' views on language study, and that most schools were not, in any case, equipped to deliver high quality vocational language skills (Lawes, 2000). Seeking a compromise, Hawkins (2005), rather than favouring one rationale over the other, proposed a stage-based pedagogical model, permitting students to experience both, while moving progressively towards utilitarian purposes.

The 2000s also saw an increasing focus on language education for the purpose of social cohesion and integration. Like other academics, Pachler (2002) and Mitchell (2003) called for language learning to be better linked to citizenship and pluricultural education, in order to foster social cohesion in our increasingly multilingual and culturally diverse communities – a call that has since been echoed multiple times (Newby et al., 2009) and generally receives less criticism than either of the instrumental or educational range of arguments. However, concerns over its execution in practice, and its feasibility within formal educational settings more generally, are frequently expressed. Williams (2001: 47), for instance, remarked that in most classrooms, the aim of global citizenship in language education tends to amount to 'symbolic virtue signalling'.

More overtly political rationales, such as national and international cohesion, diplomacy and security (e.g. Mitchell, 2003; LLAS, n.d.), also came to the fore in the 2000s. In the US, politicisation of language education was fuelled by the events of 9/11. Kramsch (2005) described the increasing demand by the US government for speakers with advanced levels of language proficiency to serve the needs of national security, specifically intelligence and military purposes. Increasingly, so Kramsch, language is seen as possessing an exchange value, with LEP and language pedagogy needing to adapt to a fast-changing world.

> Through its mobility of people and capital, its global technologies and its global information networks, globalisation has changed the conditions under which FLs [foreign languages] are taught, learned, and used. It has destabilised the codes, norms, and conventions that FL educators relied upon to help learners be successful users of the language once they had left their classrooms. These changes call for a more reflective, interpretive, historically grounded, and politically engaged pedagogy than was called for by the communicative language teaching of the eighties. (Kramsch, 2014: 312)

The LEP of the European Union has been characterised by its political engagement ever since its conception, strongly focusing on citizenship education, social cohesion and intercultural communication skills (Newby et al., 2009). 'Multilingualism is part and parcel of both European identity/citizenship and the learning society' (European Commission, 1995: 47).

Finally, a still more overtly political anchoring still can be found in the notion of a 'patriotic' rationale, expressed here with exemplary clarity by a group of Russian academics:

> Teaching a foreign language in a modern Russian school gives the teacher ample opportunities to educate citizenship, patriotism, legal culture, and high moral qualities of the individual. This is facilitated by the communicative orientation of the subject, its appeal to the study of life, customs, traditions and, above all, the language of another people. The study of a foreign culture through the language becomes possible only on the basis of the formed national-cultural base of the native language. Any knowledge acquired through a foreign language will be perceived only through the prism of knowledge formed in the process of mastering the native culture. (Larina et al., 2020: 350)

Here, justifications for language study are politicised somewhat differently to Western LEP documents (e.g. of the EU) in (at least) two respects: patriotism, in the sense used by Larina and colleagues (2020), that is, of the individual serving the interests of the nation, is superimposed on other rationales. Secondly, L2 learning is not to serve the *rapprochement* to foreign cultures but to appreciate *foreign* cultures 'through the prism of knowledge formed in the process of mastering the native culture'. This stands in stark contrast to rationales for language learning explicitly aiming to foster an international outlook and *international posture* (Ushioda, 2017), as, for instance, the European LEP (EU fact sheet on the European Union: Language Policy).

Section 4 returns to the notions of 'patriotism' and 'international posture', but this time from the perspective of student motivation. For now, the discussion of political rationales for language learning concludes with the remark that they can be more or less overt and explicit, in both Western and non-Western contexts.

In sum, since the 2000s, the social and political dimensions of rationales of language learning have received increasing emphasis. Within the EU, development of LEP is strongly supported by the Council of Europe, with its two branches, the Language Policy Division and the European Centre for Modern Languages, offering guidelines and pedagogical and policy support (for details of policies and publications, see Extra & Yagmur, 2012). Rationalising language education with reference to sociopolitical cohesion rests on the assumptions of a strong link between language and culture, and the proposition that appreciation of diversity, international posture and cross-cultural communicative skills can be mediated via language learning. There is, by now, a large body of literature on the topic of language teaching for the purposes of international integration and social cohesion (Breidbach, 2003), in contrast to work on the notion of language teaching for national cohesion and patriotism.

3.3 Critique of Rationales for Language Learning to Date

Having sketched out how rationales for language learning developed from 'enrichment type' only – towards a more binary 'instrumental–educational' conceptualisation, and finally a more refined contemporary vision including sociopolitical dimensions – we can now address the question of how rationales might respond to the challenges of Global English. The challenges in developing a system of rationales able to withstand the 'lure' of Global English, are threefold.

3.3.1 Focus on Material Benefits

The popularity of English as L2 has reinforced the focus on *utilitarian justifications* for language study. This focus can lead to the erroneous impressions that material benefits trump other benefits of language learning, and moreover, that non-utilitarian rationales are best suited for the study of LOTE (Graham, 2022) rather than English. However, it remains questionable whether school education systems are best equipped to teach languages for such purposes. Most importantly, a focus on utilitarian benefits can damage rationales and motivation for LOTE learning – not because these benefits do not exist, but because they remain poorly understood, and furthermore because learners themselves remain sceptical that school education alone can equip them with sufficient language skills for such purposes (Lanvers & Chambers, 2019).

3.3.2 Lack of Appreciation of Non-material Rationales

The 'educational' and 'enrichment' type arguments for language study remain rather underdeveloped in many LEPs, both conceptually and pedagogically. Intellectually, the EU contributions on the topic articulate one of the most comprehensive conceptions of non-material rationales, moreover, one that can be applied to learning LOTE as well as English. So far, few attempts have been made by educators and education systems to communicate such contemporary rationales to key stakeholders, notably learners themselves, and their parents, so that they might influence learner motivation. To achieve the European objectives of valuing any language learning and multilingual skills in a large variety of languages, however, engaging stakeholders in these non-utilitarian rationales is vital.

3.3.3 Misunderstanding Political Rationales

No LEP is developed in a vacuum: all emerge within their sociopolitical contexts and needs, and the mere existence of political dimensions in LEP cannot be framed as positive or negative per se. Language education policy can be harnessed for a whole range of political purposes, and LEPs purportedly 'free' of political interest fail to acknowledge their sociopolitical embedding. A more genuine way forward would be to encourage discourses concerning the political engagement of LEP and increase transparency and democracy in LEP planning. At its most basic level, it should include engaging stakeholders such as learners themselves in discussions on the sociopolitical benefits of language study.

In sum, the popularity of English as L2 obliges educators and policymakers to reconsider how to safeguard diversity in language learning, that is, a diverse body of students learning a diversity of languages. Past emphasis on material benefits of any language study has been somewhat unhelpful in two respects: (inadvertently) denigrating LOTE and downplaying non-material benefits of language study. The matrix presented in Section 3.4 seeks to address this.

3.4 A Twenty-First Century Matrix for Language Learning Rationales

The questions *Why learn languages?* and *Why make students learn languages?* can be interpreted in (at least) two different ways: *What kinds of benefits does it bring (nature of benefit)?* and *Who exactly benefits (beneficiary)?* Both questions have been addressed in a variety of ways in different conceptualisations of rationales (see Section 3.2) but have not been encapsulated in this format before. Taking the two dimensions *beneficiary* and *nature of benefit*, the range of rationales can be conceptualised on a two-axis matrix, rather than, as common hitherto, as dichotomous. Both dimensions are conceptualised not as binary but as continua. The following presents a novel matrix of rationales, suitable for and beyond the age of Global English, which spans, on one level, material and non-material and, on the other, societal and individual benefits. This matrix design emphasises

- the interdependence of different benefits for language learning
- the sociopolitical dimension of language learning
- the shortcomings of utilitarian rationales alone

and aims to help language education policymakers and educators to both design and communicate rationales to key stakeholders.

This section presents these two dimensions as part of one unified matrix for rationales for language learning. Figure 1 shows this matrix, with, on the Y axis, the dimension of *beneficiary*, and on the X axis, *nature of benefits*.

The matrix serves heuristic purposes: it is designed to help policymakers and educators to *consider* the widest possible range of rationales for language learning before deciding on their own emphasis. It offers a framework in

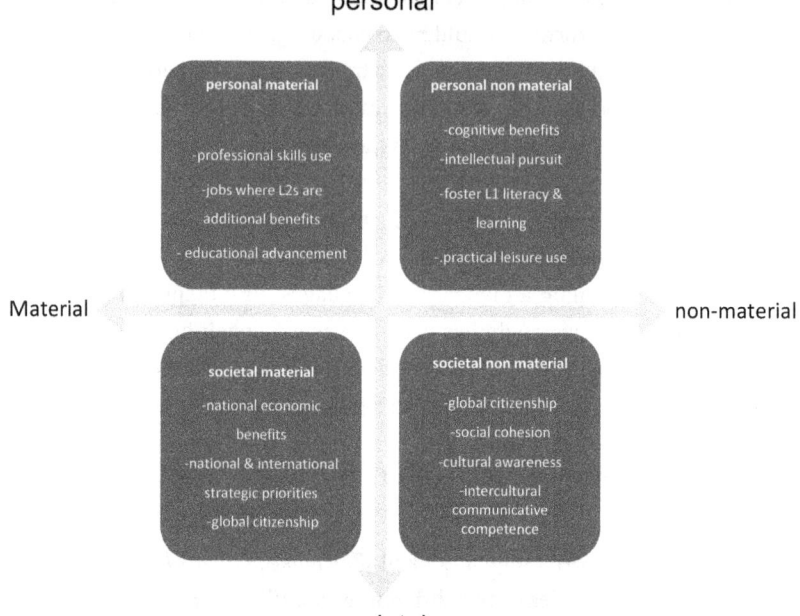

Figure 1 Matrix: holistic rationales for language teaching.

which different LEPs can situate the rationales suitable for their specific contexts. In other words, the matrix offers a sufficient level of abstraction to situate the full range of existing rationales.

The matrix does not suggest a hierarchy of rationales, nor does it ineluctably lead to suggestions regarding target languages, target learners or target competence levels. The matrix is designed to equip key stakeholders with the means to better formulate policies answering to the challenges of language learning in the context of Global English, and to communicate these to all concerned. Section 3.4.1 expands on the dimensions *beneficiary* and *nature of benefit*, and the four corners emerging from this matrix.

3.4.1 Dimension: Nature of Benefits

This continuum has, in the past, often been labelled *personal enrichment versus functional purposes*. Before mass education (McLelland, 2018), this dimension also aligned to a large extent with elite education, with the 'personal enrichment' range of arguments reserved for elite learners. Today, this association would be regarded as unacceptable by many policymakers, as it does not align with meritocratic or democratic understandings of education. Furthermore, from a humanist perspective, the ever increasing body of research underpinning the scope of cognitive benefits deriving from language learning (Bak, 2016) would mandate comprehensive rather than selective language learning. Twenty-first century research in psycholinguistics has given prominence to this range of arguments for language study – a phenomenon that has yet to translate fully into LEP.

Regarding the range of material benefits, within the context of Global English, utilitarian conceptualisation of language systems would lead most education systems to focus on English, at the expense of LOTE. If using purely utilitarian arguments for language study, the cost–benefit exercise of 'return on investment' of any language education would inevitably reinforce existing language hierarchies and favour languages with the highest Q values. As things currently stand, this would favour English in non-anglophone contexts, and other world languages in anglophone contexts. Such rationales alone would not safeguard diversity in language education.

Further drawbacks of these rationales concern the limited scope to motivate learners. Learners may justifiably query the evidence for the utilitarian benefits of learning a particular language, especially if, as is often the case in education systems, they have no choice over the target language offered, which might, moreover, be of a lesser Q value than languages with which they are already familiar. In the UK, educators who tried to incentivise language learners with materialist and utilitarian arguments have done so to little effect (Lanvers & Graham, 2022), because learners imbued in an 'English is enough' mentality (Lanvers, 2017b) are not easily convinced by material arguments. A further problem specific to anglophone contexts is the extent to which chauvinistic linguistic attitudes (such as 'English is enough') remain stubbornly anchored in the lower stratum of socioeconomic background (Coffey, 2018; Lanvers, 2017b). Now, we turn to the question *Who benefits from language learning?*

3.4.2 Dimension: Beneficiaries

In this matrix of rationales, societal benefits are given equal weight to individual ones. The matrix also assumes that both society at large and the individual may profit from material and non-material benefits, to similar measures. Concerning personal non-material benefits, new findings on the range of cognitive benefits of language learning and multilingualism (Bak, 2016), going beyond access to high culture, or practical benefits when on a leisure trip abroad, have invigorated this dimension. The material range of rationales, such as professional and educational advancement, are often cited as reasons for learners to learn or continue a language (Lanvers, 2017b; 2018b), arguments that align with a utilitarian understanding of language learning.

Turning to the dimension of societal benefits of language learning, hitherto, material arguments have tended to receive more attention than non-material ones, especially outside academia. The need for language for commerce and trade, for diplomacy and security (including military intelligence, i.e. spying), to improve trade and plan for national and international strategic needs are often cited (e.g. Fidrmuc & Fidrmuc, 2016; Foreman-Peck & Wang, 2014), in both anglophone and non-anglophone contexts. Politically, these rationales align with a utilitarian 'return on public investment' argument. Theoretically, such arguments could serve to justify a range of LOTE learning so long as a case can be made for their usefulness for specific contexts (Gazzola, 2016; Grin, 2008).

I now turn to the most overlooked dimension to date, in most contexts of LEP except for that of the EU: non-material benefits for social entities such as nations. As advocates of the pedagogy of intercultural communicative competence have long argued (Byram, 2008a, 2008b), learners with access to several languages and cultures are likely to have a better understanding and open-mindedness towards differences, and thus make a positive contribution to social cohesion (Hazel, 2016). In a similar vein, multilingual speakers tend to be better equipped than monolinguals to develop their competencies in global citizenship, using a variety of means (including social media) to engage with different cultures around the globe (Byram & Wagner, 2018). For some decades now, the learning aims of the CEFR have included goals beyond skills mastery and L2 knowledge (CEFR, 2020). In addition to valuing cultural diversity, openness and respect towards others, fairness and democratic processes are cornerstone aims of the CEFR (Byram, 2022). Developing active citizenship is also as key to the CEFR goals as language skills and knowledge itself. Furthermore, language learning is conceptualised as a lifelong process of developing plurilingual skills (Trim, 2002).

What sets apart this range of non-material benefits from others is its comprehensive scope, in two senses. *All* learners could benefit from these equally well, regardless of future professional, educational trajectory, social background and so on. They are also comprehensive in that they encompass a range of political, attitudinal and psychological dimensions.

Rationales of this nature do not align easily with utilitarian conceptualisations of language. They do, however, align well with a set of contemporary sociolinguistic frameworks in applied linguistics and second language acquisition (SLA): the social turn (Block, 2003), the multilingual turn in language education (Coneth & Meier, 2014) and the translanguaging turn (Wei, 2018). All three share the notions of social embeddedness of language learning and language use, and the fluency of language boundaries. A socially embedded conceptualisation of language skills and language learning inherently includes

Language Learning beyond English 41

the social benefits of language learning, such as intercultural understanding, openness to *otherness*, respect and increased social cohesion. Such societal attitudes can aid diplomacy, reduce sectarian and racial tension and in extreme cases even help avoid disaster or war (Kramsch, 2014). Although such benefits may be harder to measure than purely economic benefits, they can nonetheless be tangible (Ramadhan et al., 2019). These rationales lend themselves to advocating the learning of languages of relevance for the specific societal context: community languages, languages of neighbours, heritage languages, rather than globally dominant languages.

The exercise of scrutinising the matrix of rationales against the 'English is enough' fallacy and English dominance in language learning has revealed material rationales to be more vulnerable than non-material ones. It may be surprising, then, that even though de Swaan and Phillipson share utilitarian conceptualisations of language systems, they draw different conclusions regarding the 'danger' of English dominance. De Swaan, from an individualistic stance, underlines the aspirational and self-improving potential of the language, while Phillipson, from a collectivist stance, underlines the deleterious effects on other languages and cultures. Neither can be described as neutral (Hult, 2017), and neither do justice to language learning as a holistic endeavour. Utilitarian rationales turn questions of language learning into an economic cost-benefit calculation. Decisions as to how many should learn which language, and to what level, would depend on the return on educational investment: this is likely to be only a minimal investment, to benefit just the number of people necessary to reap the desired benefits, focusing on learning languages with a high Q value. In sum, utilitarian conceptualisations of language systems are ill suited to promote the learning of LOTE – especially if they are perceived to be of little use, and utilitarian rationales contain both the threat of elitism in language learning and a threat to the learning of small languages.

The opposite picture emerges when scrutinising non-utilitarian rationales: all personal enrichment rationales are – conceptually at least – accessible to *all* learners, underscoring a mandate to offer language study as comprehensively as possible. Furthermore, the benefits move seamlessly between the individual and societal dimensions: the more individuals reap the benefit of, for example, increased tolerance and intercultural understanding, the more society as a whole might benefit.

In sum, the exercise of scrutinising rationales concludes that the presence of a dominant global language does not need to threaten rationales for LOTE learning. For the learner of English, neither the material to non-material continuum nor the personal–societal continuum presents itself with a dilemma: by learning one language, a whole range of benefits can be reaped at once.

Moreover, many of these benefits could be attainable even at low or intermediate proficiency levels. The reverse can be said for the anglophone language learner: material rationales are vulnerable to the 'English is enough' fallacy, while non-material rationales present policymakers and learners with the conundrum of which language to learn, to what level, by how many students, and so on. Both comprehensive and compulsory learning of a L2 can be justified in anglophone education contexts, but to do so, most language education policymakers will need to embrace wider educational and humanistic rationales for language learning rather than just material ones.

3.5 From Rationales to Motivation

This section discusses how and if rationales might be translatable into motivational arguments and incentives for learners. The observation that rationales tend to be poorly expressed and communicated to learners constitutes only one (smaller) problem in this context. Even if rationales were devised and communicated in a convincing way to learners, the issue remains that these rationales were selected *for* learners, not *by* them. Learner motivation, and the conditions under which learners may become motivated, are very complex social psychological phenomena (Lanvers, 2017a; Ushioda, 2012). Motivational influences span from the macro level of learner experiences, such as societal attitudes to language learning, to the micro level, such as liking a particular teacher or the class atmosphere.

For a systematic analysis of overlaps between rationales and motivational dimensions, a conceptual model of language learner motivation is needed. Self determination theory, a motivational theory widely applied to the language learning context, serves this purpose. It is preferred over other well-known theories in language learning motivation because (1) its extrinsic–intrinsic continuum echoes the material–non-material dimension of the matrix presented here, and (2) as a general psychological motivational theory, it lends itself to applicability across a wide range of language learning contexts.

3.5.1 Self Determination Theory

Self determination theory (Deci & Ryan, 2000) originates from psychology rather than education. Self determination theory assumes that the need for individual agency is a central motivational force, and that any external pressures to learn may be internalised by learners to different degrees, depending on how much these external forces respond to individual learner needs. Motivation is thus driven by the meeting of three closely related universal psychological needs (Ryan & Deci, 2017).

Language Learning beyond English 43

A core human need is a sense of *competence*, that is, the ability to attain outcomes, and the ability to address these in an efficacious manner. Seeking out new challenges is part of a need for growth as a human and is central to intrinsic motivation. Deci and Ryan (2000) postulate that intrinsic motivation begins with a proactive organism: humans are said to possess a natural tendency to engage in activities that they find interesting and that, in turn, promote growth. Such activities are characterised by novelty and by optimal challenge (Deci & Ryan, 2000).

A further core human need is that of *relatedness*, that is, the need to develop secure and satisfying social connections with others. In language learning, relatedness can be experienced in communication with the target language community, with peer learners and educators and/or relating to the content and topics being taught.

Thirdly, the need for *autonomy* is the desire to self-initiate and self-regulate (Deci & Ryan, 2000). In language learning, a sense of ownership over one's learning, freedom in some learning activities and self-management of learning are the vital elements for positive learner motivation. Motivation is fostered by engaging in activities that are personally meaningful and related to one's values, permitting 'identified' or intrinsic regulation. Learning contexts and activities that support learners' need for autonomy and align with their internal values and needs strengthen motivation (Noels et al., 2019).

Just like the dimensions of the rationales matrix presented earlier, the psychological dimensions of SDT are conceptualised as a continuum, which extend from more self-determined (intrinsic) to more controlled (extrinsic) regulation. Five distinct categories along this continuum are described: external regulation (motivation coming entirely from external sources such as rewards or threats); introjected regulation (externally imposed rules that students accept as norms they should follow in order not to feel guilty); identified regulation (engaging in an activity because the individual values it highly and sees its usefulness); integrated regulation (involving choiceful behaviour that is fully assimilated with the individual's other values, needs and identity); and pure intrinsic regulation (highly autonomous, engaging in behaviour purely out of interest).

Applying SDT to the task of motivating students, effective pathways would include offering students every opportunity to enhance their sense of competence (e.g. making goals attainable), experience relatedness (e.g. positive classroom atmosphere, contact to target language speakers) and autonomy (giving students some choice and freedom in learning). On the other hand, attempts to manipulate learners' classroom behaviour through extrinsic motivators (e.g. entertaining activities, reward systems, excessive praise) might promote short-term compliance but would not foster the kind of intrinsic motives and internalised goals needed to sustain the learning activity.

3.5.2 Rationales and Motivation: Overlaps

Having sketched SDT, this section turns to the question of if and how rationales for language learning, as discussed in the matrix previously, might help motivate learners. Such endeavours may seem unpromising, as rationales are logically conceptualised, usually devised top-down, and designed to meet whatever needs policymakers have identified for any specific society. Motivation, however, is based on individual experience and includes many dimensions at the micro level. For instance, no overarching rationale could ever hope to change a learner's negative experiences of relatedness in the classroom, such as 'not liking the classmates' (Lamb et al., 2019). Many emotional motivational factors at the level of the learner experience (Dörnyei, 2019) cannot be mapped onto rationales. Thus, attempts to harness rationales for motivational purposes should build on motivational dimensions that overlap with rationales to some extent and thus ask if any rationales for language learning conventionally cited might indeed respond to basic human needs. In other words, this section examines if and how any basic psychological needs might be found in the four corners of the matrix of rationales described previously.

Starting with the *personal non-material* corner of the matrix, SDT would predict that many rationales found here, such as offering a cognitive challenge, satisfying curiosity for other cultures and so on, can meet the basic needs of autonomy, competence and relatedness. A sense of competence if the learner feels they are making satisfactory progress and receiving an optimal cognitive challenge, autonomy if the language choice, learning methods and context permit the learner some self determination and relatedness if the learner can engage meaningfully with target language speakers as well as peer learners.

Furthermore, rationales in the *personal-material corner* of the matrix also can meet learner needs in terms of competence, such as experiencing a sense of fulfilment if language learning helps the individual to progress professionally or educationally. Rationales benefiting the individual, then, lend themselves to be linked to basic human needs, and thus offer a motivational potential.

For the range of *societal* rationales *(material as well as non-material)* to have any motivational potential, however, the learner would, at a minimum, need to recognise the interconnection between their individual needs and those around them. Altruism, overt moral stances or a degree of social conscience are not always a necessary step towards this: an individual may, for instance, appreciate the societal benefits that language learning brings to foster diplomacy, peace and security – for the more selfish reasons of feeling more protected themselves. To date, despite the vast literature on language learning motivation, there is little research on this aspect of motivation. There is, however, evidence that a minority of learners are indeed motivated by an altruistic desire to (re)shape their community and public attitudes to languages: such arguments respond to the *non-material societal* corner of the matrix. Section 4 discusses this specific case ('rebellious' learner motivation, Lanvers, 2016b) in more detail. Overall, the notion that language learners can be motivated by the desire to contribute to societal goods has barely entered the language learning motivation research agenda.

In sum, despite some caveats, the exercise of matching language learning rationales to core human needs that motivate learners has revealed significant overlaps. As previously argued (Lanvers & Graham, 2022), language policy can be shaped in such a way as to address basic human needs, but the challenge remains to utilise LEP effectively for motivational purposes. Most overlaps between rationales and motivation concern *personal* rather than *societal* dimensions. A hitherto overlooked opportunity for educators and policymakers to motivate learners lies in offering pathways for learners to engage with the societal range of rationales, both cognitively and emotionally. Educators often struggle to formulate these arguments, especially to demotivated learners (Thorner & Kikuchi, 2019). Learners, including those in anglophone contexts, can nonetheless engage positively with such arguments (Lanvers, 2020), as argued in Section 4.

3.6 Section Summary

Hitherto, the full range of language learning rationales had not been conceptualised in any single model. The matrix of rationales presented here is structured around the two dimensions *beneficiary* and *nature of benefit* and highlights the continuum nature of all dimensions. The matrix spans the widest possible range of rationales for language study, is applicable to many learner contexts and underscores the sociopolitical dimension in all formal state LEP planning.

Although the full range of rationales remains – theoretically – available to most learners, the context of Global English has made it harder for LEP planners and learners to engage with all rationales. In the presence of a dominant lingua franca, LEP makers may feel obliged to take a stance vis-à-vis Global English. One unhelpful consequence of this is to associate certain rationales with certain target languages (e.g. material rationales for English, 'personal enrichment' for Italian). It is hoped that the matrix presented here will help to overcome such associations.

Today's language learning contexts, however, are shaped by such perceptions, which results in learners of LOTE and English starting on an unequal footing. Already in 2005, Hawkins remarked:

> 'In non-English-speaking countries the need to get English, the global language, is predictable for all children from an early age, and this has immense implications for learners' priorities and planning. Comparisons with our pupils' performance [i.e. in the UK, UL] at MFLs are meaningless' (Hawkins 2005: 5).

Such considerations help us move away from a culture of blame when discussing the anglophone's 'indisposition' to learn languages (Lanvers & Coleman, 2017). Academics in anglophone countries have been calling for a 'new rationale for language learning in an English-speaking society' (Dearing & King, 2007: 17) for some time. However, to date, anglophone countries have largely failed to formulate a coherent case for the non-material range of rationales, both on a personal level (Coffey & Wingate, 2017) and for societal benefit (Byram, 2008). Nonetheless, the 'soft skills' benefiting communities and societies, such as international communicative competence, are receiving increasing attention, as observed by Jakubiak (2020: 214).

> global citizenship is increasingly a curricular goal of Northern educational institutions . . . . College and university learning objectives commonly include such aims as 'building global awareness'; 'fostering intercultural understanding'; and 'promoting global competencies'.

Be that as it may, however, these remain somewhat overlooked in anglophone contexts.

The social turn in language learning (Block, 2003) has widened the path for a socially embedded understanding of learner motivation (Ushioda, 2012) and facilitated a perception of language learning motivation at the level of group characteristics rather than the individual. For instance, a special issue of the *Modern Language Journal* (Ushioda & Dörnyei, 2017) addressed motivational characteristics and challenges for learners of LOTE, while Lanvers et al. (2021) discussed motivational challenges for learners with English L1 learners.

So long as we conceptualise language learning motivation as a fluid, dynamic and social phenomenon (Dörnyei, 2019), we also embrace the notion that we can influence it. Using rationales to influence motivation is a lesser trodden path than simply focusing on classroom interaction. Nonetheless, precedents do exist.

Section 4, then, offers a discussion of motivation and rationales for different learner groups, asking *What do we know about motivational characteristics of specific learner groups?* and *Which rationales might speak most to which learner groups?* For this exercise, learner groups are defined by their relation to Global English (LOTE learner, learner with English L1 etc.). The dual purpose of this exercise is (1) to examine how vulnerable different learner groups and different motivational orientations might be to the 'English is enough' fallacy; and (2) to identify motivational pathways based on rationales for each learner group.

4 Harnessing Rationales to Foster Motivation: Meeting Learners' Needs

Exercising blanket means of attempting to motivate students regardless of grade level, gender, or individuality is ineffective. (Schwan, 2021: 80)

4.1 Introduction

In the context of formal, and often compulsory, language education, *all* motivation is welcome. The aim of this section is to discuss how rationales might be put into the service of learner motivation for different learner groups. Generic recommendations on how to motivate learners are likely to be ineffectual: any recommendations given here can only be as specific as our current knowledge of motivational characteristics at the group level.

Trying to motivate learners is one of the most effective pathways pedagogues have at their disposal to influence learning outcomes. It is thus hardly surprising that the – by now, substantial – literature on how to incentivise language learners focuses on language teaching methods and materials, teacher interaction, classroom atmosphere and similar situational variables. There is, by now, a large body of evidence on motivational teaching strategies, spearheaded by Dörnyei and Csizér (1998), which gives teachers helpful advice on how to enhance the classroom atmosphere, respond to learner needs, avoid boredom and so on. Broadly speaking, this literature focuses on teacher-initiated activity and psychological support to address learner needs. Some of these approaches have been proven effective in quasi-experimental intervention design studies (for a review, see Lanvers & Graham, 2022).

This section is organised in the following way. Section 4.2 informs about the methodology applied for this review. Sections 4.3–4.6 present our knowledge on language motivation to date and discuss how motivation might be improved, following SDT principles. This is done by learner group, depending on their relation to English, in the following way: 4.3 discusses learners of English, 4.4 learners of LOTE, 4.5 learners of LOTE with English L1, and 4.6 the amotivated learner. Section 4.7 summarises the section.

4.2 Methodological Consideration

There is by now considerable evidence of what might motivate learners, especially in the classroom (Lamb, 2019). Interventions to increase learner engagement tend to rely on influencing emotional, affective and behavioural dimensions of the learning process itself, such as improving learning strategies.

By comparison, the motivational pathway of engaging learners openly in the *why* (learn languages) debate is used to a lesser extent, but it is not entirely novel. Past intervention studies aiming to increase language learner motivation have used an array of cognitive approaches, highlighting both material (Taylor & Marsden, 2014) and non-material rationales (Forbes et al., 2021; Lanvers, 2020; Lanvers et al., 2019) to increase motivation. Large-scale interventions applied in UK educational contexts, such as *Language Horizons* and *Routes into Languages* (see Lanvers & Graham, 2022), also rely to varying degrees on such argumentative pathways.

The motivational pathways proposed here are envisioned somewhat differently, in several respects. The first observation is that motivational profiles of learners, as well as pathways to influence motivation, are conceptualised *in terms of the learner's relation to English*. Secondly, the enormous challenge of describing the motivational characteristics of learner groups on a global scale necessitates a motivational framework that is broad and comprehensive enough to conceptualise learner motivation in a large variety of contexts. For this reason, SDT, a general psychological motivational theory, is applied here. Thirdly, and in line with the core principles of SDT as a motivational framework, the motivational activities described here should not be categorised as following cognitive, social *or* emotive pathways, but rather as avenues that holistically address the core human needs of autonomy, relatedness and competence – these needs have both cognitive and emotional dimensions.

In SLA research, the person-centred turn in language learning has led to an increased emphasis on the role of emotion in language learning (Dewaele & MacIntyre, 2016). Emotions in language learning not only are important for the immediate learner environment (MacIntyre et al., 2019): they also form sociocultural and cognitive attitudes that can provide motivation for language learning (Gardner, 2010). For the same reasons, this Element refrains from a clear dichotomisation of 'conscious' and 'unconscious' motivation in language learners (Al-Hoorie, 2016a, 2016b). When adopting a holistic framework of learner motivation that gives equal emphasis to social, emotional and cognitive dimensions (MacIntyre et al., 2019), initiatives to manipulate motivation should be conceptualised holistically. Discussing rational arguments for language learning with students may seem to favour cognitive engagement, but students themselves engage with such arguments in any way they wish – that is, holistically.

The literature overviews in Sections 4.3 to 4.6 are based on empirical studies undertaken in (mainly secondary) school contexts published in peer review outlets over the last three decades. The work available to cite invariably leads to biases, as there are far fewer empirical studies from the Global South, and studies on LOTE motivation, than learners from the Global North and learners of English.

Language Learning beyond English

Furthermore, much literature on motivation may provide policymakers and practitioners with much-needed guidance as to how to incentivise learners, but empirical testing on such incentivisations also remains relatively scant. Such language learning motivational literature also has a tendency to overlook a decisive factor in language learning, namely the relation the learner has to English (L1? L2?). As argued throughout this Element, to a considerable extent, today's challenges of motivating learners present themselves differently depending on where English fits into the learning context. Dörnyei and Ushioda argue that

> we may need to adopt a two-tier approach to analysing L2 motivation, depending on whether the target language is English (as world language) or not. This is because motivation for learning English is likely to be qualitatively different in many ways from learning other second or foreign languages, as English increasingly becomes viewed as a basic educational skill to be developed from primary level alongside literacy and numeracy. (Dörnyei & Ushioda, 2021: 72)

For this reason, this section presents language learners' motivational profiles in terms of learners' relation to English. This socially grounded understanding of L2 motivation is

> 'in keeping with wider contemporary trends within the field of applied linguistics that has highlighted emergentist and dynamic systems approaches to understanding SLA' (Dörnyei & Ushioda, 2021: 72).

Sections 4.3 to 4.6 each provide a summary of the evidence on motivational makeup and motivational challenges for each learner group, followed by suggestions as to how rationales for language education might be translated into motivational pedagogy, for each of these learner groups in turn.

4.3 Learners of English

4.3.1 Dominant Motivational Characteristics

For many learners, 'English is not just a subject on the school curriculum but a passport to personal advancement' (Lamb et al., 2019: 3). Many learners feel compelled to learn the 'language that appears to have become a cog in the neoliberal wheel in the service of the global marketplace, capitalism, consumption, and national and global security' (Duff, 2017: 604). For some time now, the personal material benefits and opportunities associated with learning English have been heralded as a key argument in favour of English, more so in the Global South than the Global North (Canagarajah, 1999). Given the unquestionable status of English, rationales in the 'material personal' corner of the matrix remain the most persuasive for the learner of English.

The key observation, however, concerns the overall high motivation among many learners, covering a wide range of motivational dimensions. Reviews on the topic (Al-Hoorie, 2018; Ushioda, 2017) confirm that learners of English are not merely motivated by extrinsic rewards: both intrinsic and extrinsic motivation score highly in many learners of English. There is also evidence that learners of English who may start with a more extrinsic orientation gradually broaden their motivation to encompass a more holistic spectrum (Lamb et al., 2019), and that a motivational drop, often observed in LOTE learners, is not as marked (Lamb et al., 2019). A possible reason for these phenomena is that, in addition to any material benefits, English can facilitate access to modern culture, social media, international travel and so on. From a pedagogical perspective, such a wide spread of motivational orientations is likely to stabilise learner behaviour and to protect the learner at times when motivation dips (Kim & Kim, 2021). Summarising the evidence on motivational makeup for this learner group, Figure 2 ranks the relative salience of different motivational orientations from 1 to 4, with the darkest background shade representing the strongest for this group.

In sum, it is pleasing to see a wide spectrum of motivational orientations among many learners of English, but it leaves us with two questions: why learn any other language? Do learners engage with any societal benefits for learning English? The discussion that follows, then, asks not how rationales might be used to intensify motivation for English per se, but rather how these might be used to further motivation for LOTE and increase appreciation of the social benefits driving from the acquisition of language skills.

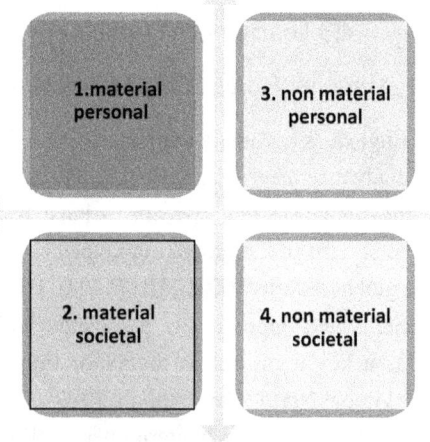

Figure 2 Motivation in learners of English.

4.3.2 Motivating Learners of English

The (scant) empirical evidence on the issue of orientating learner motivation from learning English towards LOTE is presented first. In contrast to learning English, where target communities are both fragmented and defined by neither cultural nor geographical boundaries, learners of LOTE stand a greater chance of experiencing a sense of relatedness towards the LOTE community of the target language and culture they study (Dörnyei & Al-Hoorie, 2017). Support from more advanced peer learners can also increase learners' sense of relatedness and competence (Wang, 2023). Thus, regarding the opportunity for learners to fulfil their need to *relate*, learners turning from English to LOTE can experience motivational gains in this domain (Oakes & Howard, 2022). The challenge in directing the existing (positive) motivational stances towards LOTE remains that few other languages can offer material benefits and opportunities for international communication to the same degree as English.

Given this profile, a focus on non-material benefits would best serve these learners to increase engagement with LOTE learning. Many learners of English already identify with these motivational dimensions, dimensions that furthermore do not conflict with material incentives to study English. Studies aiming to incentivise anglophone learners to learn LOTE demonstrate that learners do respond positively to awareness-raising exercises of the cognitive, personal and cultural benefits of language study (Lanvers, 2020); to date, similar approaches remain underutilised with learners of English.

Societal benefits are often the most difficult arguments to convey to learners, not only on account of their more conceptual nature but also because they presume that many individuals do possess a minimum of social conscience or altruism. This assumption is generally accepted in SDT, given an individual's desire to relate to others (Xu & Chen 2016). To date, there is little empirical research on this issue, but there is evidence that for learners of English, appreciation of this type of motivation varies between cultures. For instance, Kouritzin and colleagues (2009) found that students in cultures with more collectivist orientations such as Japan appreciated the social benefits of language skills more than those from more individualistically oriented cultures, such as Canada or France.

Finally, the notion of 'patriotic motivation' is currently discussed in the contexts of Japan, China and Russia only (Gao, 2011; Rivers, 2011; Zhang & Kim, 2013). Zhang and Kim (2013: 660) define patriotic motivation, somewhat circularly, as 'the student desire to use language learning to fulfil a patriotic desire', and do not expand on the possible provenance of such desires. So far, the concept of patriotic motivation has not been applied in learner contexts and education systems outside cultures with a strong collectivist orientation: its precise nature and existence thus remain imprecise, especially in Western contexts. Within L2 motivational research, attempts to harness any social and altruistic motivation for such explicit ideological purposes remain marginalised.

It is important to concede that even in highly collectivist-oriented cultures, learners have autonomy to engage differently with such motivational dimensions. Learners are not products of their social environment 'but also active producers of their own social and cultural environments' (Dörnyei & Ushioda, 2021: 34), and thus may engage very differently with the somewhat conceptual notion of patriotic motivation. Except for the few above-mentioned studies, there are no empirical studies on individual differences in terms of 'patriotic' motivational orientation to date.

As discussed in Section 3, *international posture*, a somewhat different collective motivational orientation, describes 'personal interest in foreign or international affairs ... and openness or a non-ethnocentric attitude toward different cultures' (Yashima, 2002: 57). Among learners of English, international posture is a well established, and often strong, motivational orientation. Comparative research on multilingual researchers has shown that learners of both English and LOTE can demonstrate high international posture in both target languages (Siridetkoon, 2015). Thus, the potential exists for extending international posture in learning English towards LOTE, especially for those learning other world languages.

To conclude, to strengthen motivation in learners of English and simultaneously diversify their motivation towards other languages, non-material benefits (both societal and personal) should be highlighted.

4.4 Learners of LOTE

4.4.1 Dominant Motivational Characteristics

If Global English features as neither L1 nor L2, that is, where a LOTE L1 speaker is learning a LOTE, the nature of the motivational make-up for learning depends even more on the precise situatedness of the learner context than for learners of English (Zhen et al., 2019). The combination of language constellations is endless. Pedagogues who might have hoped that the absence of English offers LOTE learners opportunities to develop motivational profiles unaffected by Global English will be disappointed. Many learn English as their first L2, an experience bound to influence the LOTE learner. For better or for worse, past experiences of learning English shape attitudes, motivation and expectations in their LOTE learning (Henry, 2010), and LOTE motivation often suffers, regardless of whether English is learned simultaneously or consecutively (Henry, 2012). Studies by Henry in particular (Henry & Apelgren, 2008) demonstrate how English as first L2 can add to disillusionment regarding learners' expectations of the ultimate proficiency they might achieve in their LOTE, a negative motivational dimension often growing as long as the student studies the LOTE formally at school. This is one of several ways in which English can have a negative impact on LOTE motivation (Mendoza & Phung, 2019), an unsurprising observation given the emphasis on English in most education systems (Duff, 2017).

Figure 3 ranks the motivational orientations of LOTE learners from 1 to 3 (material motivations sharing bottom place), with more salient rationales again in deeper shading.

The first observation is represented by the lack of deep shading: overall LOTE learners face more motivational challenges than those of English. Conceptually at least, non-material individual rationales are relatively neutral as to the L2: they could help motivate the learning of LOTE. The evidence, however, is that many students themselves do not share this view: when comparing intrinsic ranges of motivation in those learning a LOTE and English simultaneously, they often show higher intrinsic motivation for English than for LOTE (Sugita et al., 2017). Hence, this motivation orientation is labelled the most important in Figure 3. As non-material personal orientations in learners of LOTE are beginning to be better understood (Lanvers et al., 2021; Ushioda & Dörnyei, 2017), evidence suggests that the competition with English remains a threat to LOTE motivation.

On the question of whether those learning more than one LOTE simultaneously have different motivational profiles for each target language or not, the

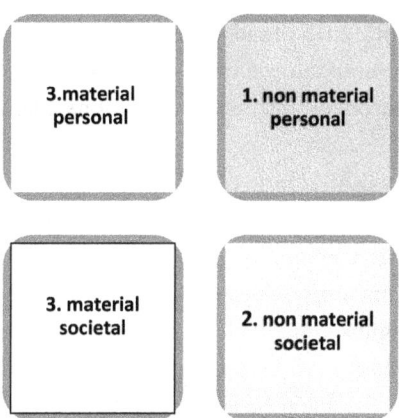

Figure 3 Motivation in LOTE learners.

jury is still out, with some studies suggesting that students may develop discrete motivational 'selves' (Duff, 2017: 599) for different target languages (Liu & Oga-Baldwin, 2022) or interrelated ones (Henry, 2017; Huang, 2019). To date, most studies seem to suggest that motivational make-up is different for different L2s (Nakamura, 2019), but studies comparing motivation between those learning LOTE and English simultaneously tend to report higher material motivation for English than for LOTE (Huang, 2019).

Furthermore, there is evidence that in Asian (unlike in Western) contexts, material and non-material orientations may be similar for both LOTE and English (Huang et al., 2015; Kong et al., 2018). Recent studies (e.g. Zheng et al., 2019) also suggest that intrinsically motivated students of several languages have a more 'multilingual' identity, while more extrinsically motivated learners favour English alone. Generally, however, cross-linguistic research on motivational profiles is an emerging research field (Nakamura, 2019). Concerning the question of whether LOTE learners might be incentivised by a wider range societal benefits deriving from language learning, we observe again a lack of empirical studies.

In sum, learners perceive the material benefits of learning LOTE to be lower than for English (Huang, 2019; Henry, 2010): they are labelled as least important in Figure 3. Prior experience of learning English often has a detrimental motivational effect on LOTE learning. These results come with the caveat that most evidence on motivation for LOTE learning stems from learners of the large European languages and Chinese. Findings suggest a need to differentiate between European and Asian studies, in that Asian students often show themselves to be equally strongly intrinsically and extrinsically motivated, and for the educated elite especially, extrinsic motivation can be very strong. On the other hand, European studies (e.g. Henry & Cliffordson, 2013) tend to report more gender differences than those investigating motivation among Asian students, with Western girls tending to report stronger intrinsic orientations than boys (Menzoda & Phung, 2019).

Finally, Dörnyei and Al-Hoorie (2017) summarise characteristics of LOTE learner motivation as having great resilience, and a great sense of relatedness to the target language community, often accompanied by very specific personal motivation. This profile does indeed describe a specific LOTE learner type: that of the highly motivated LOTE learner, including the rebellious learner, which I discuss next. Unfortunately, however, many LOTE learners start from a low motivational base. The most salient feature of the LOTE learner motivational profile is poorer motivation compared to that for learning English.

4.4.2 Motivating LOTE Learners

Research on how motivation for English might be extended to the learning of LOTE is in its infancy and lacks empirical studies. The most complete articulation of the vision for a unified multilingual motivation profile can be found in an edited Element by Dörnyei and colleagues (2015), exploring theoretical and methodological options for how to develop *one* holistic multilingual motivational learner profile. Evidence to date, however, suggests that motivation for English tends to compete with that for LOTE, and, given that most learners perceive a 'higher return on investment' with English, and also tend to experience English as their first L2, motivation for LOTE starts somewhat on the back foot – a drawback that can only be countered by a greater validation of non-material rationales. Attempts to change motivational profiles in this learner group thus should focus on fostering whatever non-material personal motivation can be kindled and extended, first and foremost to non-material societal motivation (currently second-most salient in this group). In this way, the matrix can offer clear pathways and pedagogical direction for incentivising learner groups with different needs and challenges

4.5 Learners of LOTE with English L1

4.5.1 Dominant Motivational Characteristics

Undertaking the same exercise of testing the vulnerability of rationales for this learner group to the attraction of English, a picture emerges whereby most rationales 'suffer' somewhat from English dominance. Figure 4 shows, again using shading and numbering by relative importance, how the motivational make-up looks for a LOTE learner who already speaks English as (one of their) L1s, according to current evidence on learner attitudes and motivation: non-material motivation outranks material.

Figure 4 shows even less shading (i.e. overall lower motivation) than in Figure 3. For learners who already know English, motivation is vulnerable to the 'English is enough' fallacy often found in anglophone countries. Anglophones face a greater initial motivational hurdle, and anglophones who are motivated tend to make a greater motivational investment than others. It would follow that such learners need to rely on high amounts of intrinsic motivation. This is borne out by evidence. Comparative analysis confirms that anglophones opting for the same L2 as non-anglophones (e.g. Brits and French both learning German) show higher motivation (Bartram, 2006). In a further defence of anglophones' attitudes towards language learning, it is important to concede that chauvinistic attitudes towards one's first language are not

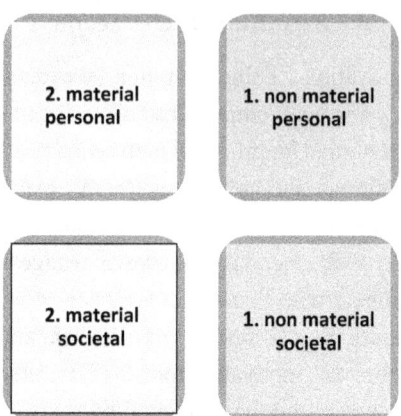

Figure 4 Motivation in LOTE learners with English L1.

a preserve of anglophones (Pratt, 2012), but such attitudes are easily fuelled by the Global English phenomenon (Lanvers et al., 2021).

Emphasising material benefits to anglophones learning LOTE may appear superficially attractive, presumably a reason why it is employed in motivational incentivisation in the UK in particular (Lanvers, 2017a). The concerns around using these arguments are not their weakness per se, but the danger that any emphasis on the material benefits of language learning could lead learners to favour English even more. If we suggest to learners that this is the main reason for language learning, they may indeed conclude that the one language offering the greatest practical functionality in many situations might suffice. In this manner, material rationales may exacerbate rather than solve motivational problems for anglophone learners (Graham, 2022).

Concerning the large range of personal non-material benefits (such as cognitive, cultural, emotional), these remain – conceptually at least – untouched by the presence of a dominant lingua franca and are suitable for a wide range of LOTE, although a learner may of course decide to immerse herself into a particular language due to a perceived cultural affinity with the target community (Stolte, 2015). The issue here is that such arguments seem harder to communicate to learners, and that any LOTE offered to learners would need its own unique rationale. How, then, to choose between French and Italian on the grounds of cultural enrichment or cognitive challenge? For the English L1 learner, the sense of overwhelming choice among L2s can be intimidating or lead to inertia. In some cases, specific non-utilitarian arguments may favour a particular target language, such as Latin for cultural enrichment, a typologically very different language for a high cognitive challenge (e.g. Chinese) and so on. Nonetheless, from the perspective of the anglophone learner, enrichment-type arguments alone seem to harbour an element of arbitrariness in the L2 choice.

This differs when considering *societal non-material benefits*: specific LOTE can address specific societal needs, such as learning a community language to improve social cohesion and social justice (Busse et al., 2020), a language of the neighbouring country to improve binational relations, or heritage language to preserve the culture of the community (Hélot et al., 2018). We now have a considerable body of literature on beneficial effects of community language teaching for schools and their neighbourhood (ECML, n.d.). Such arguments offer anglophones living in multilingual communities[2] the opportunity to engage with the immediate benefits (rather than deferred benefits, e.g. studying for a professional advancement) of language study. These arguments remain unaffected by Global English and lend themselves especially well to be used for anglophones who show little interest in language learning. To date, however, these arguments have received little attention in anglophone contexts (Osborn, 2006).

Finally, more than for any other learner group, the literature on motivation in anglophone language learners reports stark differences along sociodemographic variables, in that girls and learners from advantaged societal backgrounds report significantly higher motivation (Coffey, 2018; Lanvers, 2017b; Williams et al., 2002).

4.5.2 Motivating Anglophone Learners of LOTE

It follows from the profile in Figure 4 that anglophones learning any LOTE would benefit from emphasising the non-material benefits (both personal and societal) of language learning, and to link language learning to their learner's individual needs and concerns. Currently, in anglophone contexts, a combination of poor LEP provision, linguistic chauvinism and a socioculturally embedded belief that language learning is for the few, not the many (Lanvers, 2017), stop many learners with English L1 from developing such motivational profiles.

Nonetheless, such profiles exist. They have been identified, simultaneously but independently in the US (Thompson & Vásquez, 2015) and UK (Lanvers, 2016b). The 'rebellious learner' (Lanvers, 2016b) or 'anti-ought learner' (Thompson & Vásquez, 2015) is a learner who rejects the image of anglophones as 'bad at languages' and engages in LOTE learning both to combat such stereotypes and to engage with cultures with which they feel an affinity (see also Thompson, 2017). This attitude is striking because of not only an explicit

---

[2] Most anglophones live in multilingual communities today. For the UK, see Office for National Statistics (n.d.); for the US, see American Community Survey, 2008–2010.

rejection of (perceived) dominant societal attitudes but also a high personal investment into language learning: this motivational orientation shows an – overall rarely documented – combination of social conscience and investment into language learning for personal non-material benefits. If this motivational orientation seems the very opposite of 'patriotic motivation', where personal desire and societal needs for language learning align, this is because the rebellious learner has assessed the societal needs for languages differently to how the world around them has. For this learner type, the linguistic chauvinism of 'English is enough' is not only mistaken and injurious to societal wellbeing: explicit distancing from such attitudes is also a crucial part of their learner identity.

From a pedagogical perspective, such motivation is highly desirable. We know little so far about what exactly drives a minority of learners to develop this (Lanvers, 2016b), and how pedagogues might reproduce similar stances in others. It identified that learners *can*, spontaneously and voluntarily, link social awareness and conscience to a highly personal investment into language learning. To try and address the language learning crises in anglophone contexts, there is an urgent need for a research agenda to ascertain what may help learners to develop such stances, and how to pedagogically assist this, especially in the context of compulsory language learning. Thus, for this learner group, the matrix helped to formulate both a pedagogical and a research agenda.

4.6 The Amotivated Learner

4.6.1 Dominant Motivational Characteristics

It is striking that most pedagogical literature on amotivation in education focuses on physical education. In contrast to the vast literature on language learner motivation generally, studies investigating amotivation in language learning are sparse. Furthermore, although amotivation is not a prerogative of the anglophone learner, the scant evidence on the topic mainly stems from this learner group. Amotivation describes a relative absence of motivation whereby

> 'individuals do not perceive a contingency between their behaviors and outcomes, so they do not act with the intention to attain an outcome ... They begin to feel helpless and may start to question the usefulness of engaging in the activity in the first place' (Vallerand & Ratelle, 2002: 43).

Dörnyei and Ushioda (2021) distinguish between amotivation and demotivation, the latter describing reduction of motivation as a result of specific external forces, while amotivation describes unrealistic expectations, akin to the Vallerand and Ratelle (2002) notion of not perceiving a contingency between behaviours and outcome. This definition of amotivation is adopted here. For this learner profile, it seems redundant to add a figure representing the matrix of motivational orientation: all four corners would be equally poorly developed (white shading, no numbering).

Teachers often feel overwhelmed by the problems amotivated learners pose, but themselves lack understanding of how their teaching may impact on motivation (Oxford, 2001). In a meta review of demotivation, Gao and Liu (2022), observe that demotivation tends to emerge when teacher behaviour and learner needs are mismatched: at the level of learner experience, teacher behaviour and personality, class activities, materials used, class atmosphere and so on significantly contribute to demotivation. Concerning learners' individual needs, demotivation arises especially when learners lack experiences of feeling competent. Vandergrift (2005) has observed that those with the lowest grades display the strongest amotivation, but simply increasing their grades would not increase their motivation as such action would not address learners' poor self-efficacy.

In sum, although neither amotivation nor demotivation in language learning is as fully researched as motivation, evidence to date suggests that the amotivated learner feels that language learning cannot meet their core needs in terms of SDT, while the demotivated learner might disengage with language learning gradually as the learning experience has not given them a sense that the activity meets their needs. In such contexts, the challenges to connect abstract rationales to motivation are greater still. The most promising way forward for this learner group would be to ask *How can language learning meet learners' basic psychological needs in a most fundamental human sense? Do any of these needs relate to rationales?*

4.6.2 Motivating Amotivated Learners

Along with other researchers, Vandergrift (2005) emphasises the need to develop self-efficacy in amotivated learners: amotivated students tend to display fixed mindsets ('I will never be good at languages'). However, fostering a sense of autonomy, for instance by providing students with strategies to control and manage their learning (Pintrich & Johnson, 1990), is of equal importance, as is the nurturing of a sense of relatedness, both to learners among themselves and to target speaker groups. More than any other learner, the amotivated learner needs support to experience that their *personal needs* can be met via engaging in language learning. In the context of formal (often compulsory) language learning, these personal needs mostly manifest themselves as connected to the immediate environment: relating to peers and to the teachers, feeling a sense of accomplishment and having agency and personal investment in the task. Such needs are first and foremost of a non-material nature. Only when some initial motivational 'kindling' has been lit in the learner can we hope that they will 'nurture the fire' and engage with wider rationales for language learning, perhaps (but not necessarily) including those of a material nature. In line with SDT, the amotivated learner, even more than others, should be encouraged to see *personal intrinsic* value in language learning first and foremost (Graham, 2022). In sum, more than for the other learner groups, the link between amotivation and core principles of SDT inform pathways to incentivise this most difficult of learner groups.

The discussion of group learner motivational profiles (Sections 4.3–4.6) has, again and again, stressed the importance of engaging learners more with the non-material benefits of language learning, so as to develop robust and holistic motivational profiles, and foster an appreciation of the interconnectedness of all motivational dimensions.

4.7 Section Summary

This section discussed motivational profiles in different learner groups. Learners of English currently demonstrate both the widest range and most intense motivation of all learner groups. Among learners of LOTE, those with English L1 especially, motivational challenges related to Global English are evident. Here, using material arguments to foster motivation for LOTE holds the danger of encountering the 'English is enough' fallacy. Lanvers and Graham (2022: 227) remark that

> 'instrumental arguments [to increase learner motivation] offer, in SDT terms, more potential for infelicitous than felicitous effects, especially if the latter are countered with the 'everyone speaks English anyway' riposte'.

Furthermore, material rationales for enhancing motivation must be embedded in the specificity of the learner situation (for a specific target language and/or a specific purpose). However, even learners aware of the instrumental benefits of LOTE do not necessarily show higher motivation as a result (Michel et al., 2021).

The section then discussed how and if arguments for language teaching might be utilised to foster motivation, aiming for a pedagogy where 'holistic language learning rationales [are used] to motivate a wide range of learners for a wide range of languages' (Csizér & Dörnyei, 2005: 30). This exercise led, in all cases, to an emphasis on *non-material benefits*. Raising awareness of these lends itself to motivating a wide range of learners and holds no danger of being counterproductive – unlike material rationales. Overall, such benefits remain poorly formulated and communicated in educational practice – a lacuna this Element addresses.

5 Conclusion

> For some people, learning a new language is an exciting adventure into a fascinating linguistic realm and the ideal medium for exploring new cultures. For others, it feels pointless and boring, like a tedium to be endured. (Noels et al., 2019: 95)

I conclude this Element by first reflecting on what past lingua francas might tell us about the future of learning English, if anything. I then weigh up the opportunities the twenty-first century language learning landscape might offer us against our scope to withstand the 'stampede towards English'. I nonetheless finish on a cautiously upbeat outlook.

5.1 Lessons from Past Lingua Francas

To date, Englishisation in education systems continues apace. Even LEP explicitly espousing diversity in FL education often falls at the hurdle of Global English (*Current Issues in Language Planning*, 2022; Lanvers, 2024; Meyer, 2011), as students 'vote with their feet' to learn English in preference to LOTE. Historically, different languages have occupied the position of dominant lingua franca (Krzyzanowski & Wodak, 2011), but the question is if the consideration that English might one day suffer the fate of past lingua francas might impress learners sufficiently to diversify towards LOTE. Ostler (2010) predicts that technology will not only revolutionise language learning but also 'dethrone' English from its current position as the most desirable L2, superseded by languages such as Chinese, Spanish and Portuguese. For those interested in diversifying language learning, an optimistic outlook. The problem remains that the status English has reached today differs from past lingua franca in key respects: Its reach is truly global, and the digital revolution has lowered barriers (both physical and monetary) to learning this language like no lingua franca before. Caution would thus dictate that we should not overly rely on historic patterns of organic language growth and demise to predict the future of (learning) English.

5.2 Outlook

If hope to diversify language learning towards LOTE thus falls back to LEP, more is needed than top-down declared policy prescribing increased uptake of LOTE. Some researchers, such as Breidbach (2003: 89), have proposed LEPs that seek to combine the – de facto – preference for English with a plurilingual approach to education:

> If linguistic diversity can usefully be seen to counterbalance the gravitational force which emanates from English as a lingua franca, English may function as a direct mediator between participants in a discourse who would otherwise have to rely on translation. Furthermore, English already is the very linguistic means to give speakers, especially of lesser-used languages, their voice within a European public discourse. In summary, linguistic diversity and the use of English as a form of lingua franca very probably rely on each other.

This pragmatic compromise contains an Achilles heel, however. Sections 2 and 3 have cited ample evidence of official LEPs failing simply because students prefer to learn English over LOTE. Does 'counterbalancing the gravitational force' of English by giving this dominant language a mediator role not 'put the wolf among the sheep'? What guarantees that learners will show any more interest in LOTE than is currently the case?

In a dynamic understanding of LEP (Section 1), practised LEP is co-constructed by many stakeholders: learners, school management, teachers and the wider community. Ensuring their commitment to LEP aims and objectives is vital to narrow the gap between declared and practised policy. Non-compliance with declared LEP can take many forms. In its simplest form, a learner and/or their parents may decide not to follow their school's recommendations for language study, causing schools not to reach the targets set for FL engagement (Parrish & Lanvers, 2019). In England, academies and free schools – now the majority of secondary schools – are not obliged to follow the National Curriculum and are thus exempt from the obligation to teach FLs, if they wish. At its most overt, resistance to declared policy can take the form of a legal challenge (Spiegel, 2016). In other words, declared LEP can only succeed in diversifying learning towards LOTE if it takes key stakeholders on board. This Element has consistently argued that formulating and communicating holistic rationales for language learning, a task of declared policy, is necessary to narrow gaps between practised and declared LEP. First and foremost, these rationales should be communicated to learners themselves, as key stakeholders.

The next challenge, then, is to make the rationales relevant, meaningful and attractive to learners and their social environment. In other words, the rationales favoured by any LEP should speak to learner needs, as described by SDT (Section 4). This final, somewhat visionary section explains how holistic rationales can speak to learner needs. I recall that personal material rationales serve the learner's social, professional and material advancement (e.g. professional skills use, educational advancement, social capital), while personal non-material rationales (e.g. cognitive benefits, cultural enrichment, travel) serve advancements that cannot (easily) be monetised. Both rationales advance individuals, and both answer learners' individual needs for feeling competent (e.g. learning a language for the intellectual challenge, getting good grades for educational advancement) and feeling autonomous (e.g. becoming financially independent, choosing if and which language to learn). Furthermore, relatedness may also be satisfied if the learner has any intrinsic interests in or personal affinity to the target culture and community. Turning to societal benefits of language learning, the most salient basic human need addressed here is that to have meaningful relations with others. Furthermore, the sense that one makes a useful contribution to society can also satisfy the need for competence. Figure 5 illustrates the overlaps between rationales and basic human needs.

Figure 5, then, offers a vision of how to align holistic rationales for language learning with learner needs. The vision cannot bear fruit if rationales *and* the way they benefit individuals and society are not communicated and discussed with learners. In a holistic language learning pedagogy, learner needs and rationales for language need to coexist in harmony: alone, neither can hope to counter the 'stampede towards English'.

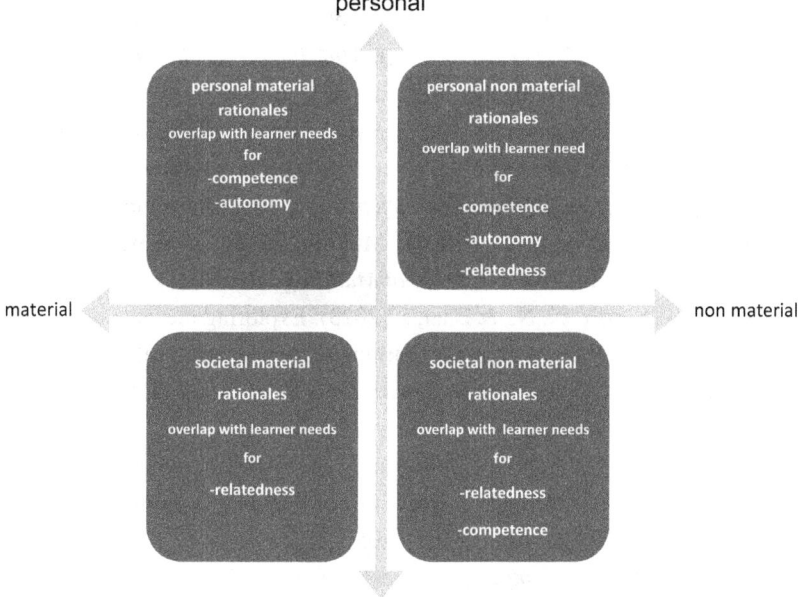

Figure 5 Situating rationales for language learning in SDT motivation.

References

Adams, J. N. (2003). 'Romanitas' and the Latin language. *The Classical Quarterly*, *53*(1), 184–205.

Adams, S. A. (2019). Translating texts: Contrasting Roman and Jewish depictions of literary translations. *Scholastic Culture in the Hellenistic and Roman Eras: Greek, Latin, and Jewish*, *2*, 147–167.

Al-Hoorie, A. H. (2016a). Unconscious motivation: Part I: Implicit attitudes toward L2 speakers. *Studies in Second Language Learning and Teaching*, *6*(3), 423–454.

Al-Hoorie, A. H. (2016b). Unconscious motivation: Part II: Implicit attitudes and L2 achievement. *Studies in Second Language Learning and Teaching*, *6*(4), 619–649.

Al-Hoorie, A. H. (2018). The L2 motivational self-system: A meta-analysis. *Studies in Second Language Learning and Teaching*, *8*(4), 721–754.

American Academy of Arts & Sciences. (2017). *America's languages: Investing in language education for the 21st century*. Accessed 10 November 2023 at www.amacad.org/publication/americas-languages.

US Census Bureau. (2011.). American Community Survey, 2008–2010. Accessed 30 April 2024 at https://bit.ly/3WrdvMW.

Aronin, L. (2006). Dominant language constellations: An approach to multilingualism studies. In M. O'Laoire (ed.), *Multilingualism in educational settings* (pp. 140–159). Schneider Publications.

Aronin, L. (2019). Dominant language constellation as a method of research. In E. Vetter & U. Jessner (eds.), *International research on multilingualism: Breaking with the monolingual perspective* (pp. 13–26). Springer.

Aronin, L., & Singleton, D. (2008). Multilingualism as a new linguistic dispensation. *International Journal of Multilingualism*, *5*(1), 1–16.

Aryadoust, V., Soo, Y. X. N., & Zhai, J. (2023). Exploring the state of research on motivation in second language learning: A review and a reliability generalization meta-analysis. *International Review of Applied Linguistics in Language Teaching*, 1–33.

Bak, T. H. (2016). The impact of bilingualism on cognitive ageing and dementia: Finding a path through a forest of confounding variables. *Linguistic Approaches to Bilingualism*, *6*(1–2), 205–226.

Baldwin, J. J. (2019). *Languages other than English in Australian higher education*. Springer.

References

Banks, J. A., Suárez-Orozco M. M., & Ben-Peretz, M. (eds.). (2016). *Global migration, diversity, and civic education: Improving policy and practice.* Teachers College Press.

Barakos, E., & Selleck, C. (2019). Elite multilingualism: Discourses, practices, and debates. *Journal of Multilingual and Multicultural Development, 40*(5), 361–374.

Bartram, B. (2006). Attitudes to language learning: A comparative study of peer group influences. *Language Learning Journal, 33*(1), 47–52.

Benson, P. (2011). *Teaching and researching autonomy in language learning* (2nd ed.). Pearson Education.

Benson, P. (2013). *Teaching and researching: Autonomy in language learning.* Routledge.

Berman, R. A. (2011). The real language crisis. *Academe, 97*(5), 30–34.

Berns, M. (2012). Lingua franca and language of wider communication. *The Encyclopedia of Applied Linguistics.* Pergamon Press.

Block, D. (2003). *The social turn in second language acquisition.* Edinburgh: Edinburgh University Press.

Bolton, K. (2019). World Englishes: Current debates and future directions. In C. L. Nelson & Z. G. Proshina (eds.), *The handbook of world Englishes* (pp. 741–760). Wiley.

Bori, P., & Canale, G. (eds.). (2002). *Critical Inquiry in Language Studies.* Special Edition *19*(4). Neoliberal foreign language education: The search for alternatives.

Bori, P., & Canale, G. (2022). Neoliberal foreign language education: The search for alternatives. *Critical Inquiry in Language Studies, 19*(4), 307–316.

Bouhours, D. (1671). *Les Entretiens d'Ariste et d'Eugene.* Accessed 4 June 2021 at https://gallica.bnf.fr/ark:/12148/bpt6k122907n/f49.item.texteImage.

Bowler, M. (2020). *A languages crisis? HEPI report 123.* Higher Education Policy Institute. Accessed 4 December 2021 at www.hepi.ac.uk/2020/01/09/a-languages-crisis/.

Bozzo, L. (2014). The multilingual context as an extrinsic motivation factor for English language learning: A case study. *Ricognizioni, 1*(1), 219–228.

Breidbach, S. (2003). European communicative integration: The function of foreign language teaching for the development of a European public sphere. *Languages for Intercultural Communication and Education, 6*, 81–91.

British Academy. (2020). *Towards a national languages strategy: Education and skills.* Accessed 10 July 2021 at www.thebritishacademy.ac.uk/publications/towards-national-languages-strategy-education-and-skills/.

British Academy, American Academy of Arts, Sciences, Academy of the Social Sciences in Australia, Australian Academy of the Humanities, & the Royal

Society of Canada. (2020). *The importance of languages in global context: An international call to action.* Accessed 10 July 2021 at www.thebritisha cademy.ac.uk/publications/the-importance-of-languages-in-global-context-an-international-call-to-action/.

British Council. (2017). *Languages for the future: Which languages the UK needs most and why.* Accessed 19 November 2017 at www.britishcouncil .org/sites/default/files/language-for-the-future-report.pdf.

British Council. (2019). *Language trends Wales.* Accessed 10 December 2023 at https://wales.britishcouncil.org/sites/default/files/language_trends_re port_final.pdf.

British Council. (2021). *Language trends in Northern Ireland.* Accessed 10 December 2023 at https://nireland.britishcouncil.org/sites/default/files/ m003_01_language_trends_ni_report_final_web_v2.pdf.

Broady, E. (2020). Language learning in the UK: Taking stock. *The Language Learning Journal, 48*(5), 501–507.

Brown, R. L. (2019). Motivations to learn languages other than English in an English-forward and technologically advanced society (Doctoral dissertation, University of Illinois at Chicago).

Bruen, J. (2021). The place of foreign languages in the Irish education system: Towards a more strategic approach. In U. Lanvers, A. Thomson, & M. East (eds.), *Language learning in anglophone countries: Challenges, practices, ways forward* (pp. 37–51). Palgrave.

Buckingham, L. (2021). Heritage language maintenance in New Zealand. In U. Lanvers, A. S. Thompson, & M. East (eds.), *Language learning in anglophone countries: Challenges, practices, ways forward* (pp. 289–307). Springer.

Bunce, P. (2012). Out of sight, out of mind ... and out of line: Language education in the Australian Indian Ocean Territory of the Cocos (Keeling) Islands. In V. Rapatahana & P. Bunce (eds.), *English language as hydra: Its impacts on non-English language cultures* (pp. 37–59). Taylor & Francis.

Burnette, J. L., Billingsley, J., Banks, G. C., Knouse, L. E., Hoyt, C. L., Pollack, J. M., & Simon, S. (2023). A systematic review and meta-analysis of growth mindset interventions: For whom, how, and why might such interventions work? *Psychological Bulletin, 149*(3–4), 174–205.

Busse, V. (2017). Plurilingualism in Europe: Exploring attitudes toward English and other European languages among adolescents in Bulgaria, Germany, the Netherlands, and Spain. *Modern Language Journal, 101*(3), 566–582.

Busse, V., Cenoz, J., Dalmann, N., & Rogge, F. (2020). Addressing linguistic diversity in the language classroom in a resource-oriented way: An intervention study with primary school children. *Language Learning, 70*(2), 382–419.

Byram, M. (2008a). *From foreign language education to education for intercultural citizenship: Essays and reflections* (Vol. 17). Multilingual Matters.

Byram, M. (2008b). The 'value' of student mobility. In M. Byram & F. Dervin (eds.), *Students, staff and academic mobility in higher education* (pp. 31–45). Cambridge Scholars Publishing.

Byram, M. (2022). Politics, origins and futures of the CEFR. *The Language Learning Journal, 50*(5), 586–599.

Byram, M., & Wagner, M. (2018). Making a difference: Language teaching for intercultural and international dialogue. *Foreign Language Annals, 51*(1), 140–151.

Calvet, L.-J. (2006). *Towards an ecology of world languages*. Polity Press.

Canagarajah, S. A. (1999). *Resisting linguistic imperialism in English language teaching*. Oxford University Press.

CEFR. (2020). Common European framework of reference for languages: Learning, teaching, assessment. Accessed 1 August 2023 at https://rm.coe.int/common-european-framework-of-reference-for-languages-learning-teaching/16809ea0d4#page=30.

Clayton, S. (2022). Systemic and personal factors that affect students' elective language other than English enrollment decisions. *Foreign Language Annals, 55*(2), 361–382.

Codó, E., & Sunyol, A. (2019). 'A plus for our students': The construction of Mandarin Chinese as an elite language in an international school in Barcelona. *Journal of Multilingual and Multicultural Development, 40*(5), 436–452.

Coffey, S. (2018). Choosing to study modern foreign languages: Discourses of value as forms of cultural capital. *Applied Linguistics, 39*(4), 462–480.

Coffey, S., & Wingate, U. (2017). Introduction. In S. Coffey & U. Wingate (eds.), *New directions for research in foreign language education* (pp. 1–7). Taylor & Francis.

Collen, I. (2020). *Language trends England 2020: British Council*. Accessed 1 August 2023 at https://pureadmin.qub.ac.uk/ws/portalfiles/portal/213540872/language_trends_2020_0.pdf.

Coneth, J., & Meier. B. (eds.). (2014). *The multilingual turn in languages education*. Multilingual Matters.

Cook V. J. (1999). 'Going beyond the native speaker in language teaching'. *TESOL Quarterly 33*, 185–209.

Copland, F., & McPake, J. (2021). 'Building a new public idea about language?': Multilingualism and language learning in the post-Brexit UK. *Current Issues in Language Planning, 23*(2), 117–136.

Council of Europe. (2020). *Common European framework of reference for languages: Learning, teaching assessment.* www.coe.int/en/web/common-european-framework-reference-languages.

Council of Europe. (n.d.). *Online platform of resources and references for plurilingual and intercultural education.* Accessed 22 May 2022 at www.coe.int/t/dg4/linguistic/langeduc/le_platformintro_EN.asp.

Cruickshank, K., Black, S., Chen, H., Tsung, L., & Wright, J. (2020). *Language education in the school curriculum: Issues of access and equity.* Bloomsbury Academic.

Csizér, K., & Dörnyei, Z. (2005). Language learners' motivational profiles and their motivated learning behavior. *Language Learning, 55*(4), 613–659.

Csizér, K., & Lukács, G. (2010). The comparative analysis of motivation, attitudes and selves: The case of English and German in Hungary. *System, 38*(1), 1–13.

Cummins, J. (2021). *Rethinking the education of multilingual learners: A critical analysis of theoretical concepts.* Multilingual Matters.

Cunningham, C. (2019). Terminological tussles: Taking issue with 'English as an additional language' and 'languages other than English'. *Power and Education, 11*(1), 121–128.

Dalby, A. (2020). *Language in danger: The loss of linguistic diversity and the threat to our future.* Columbia University Press.

Dalmau, M. S. (2020). Neoliberal language policies and linguistic entrepreneurship in higher education: Lecturers' perspectives. *Language, Culture and Society, 2*(2), 174–196.

de Swaan, A. (1993). The evolving European language system: A theory of communication potential and language competition. *International Political Science Review, 14*(3), 241–255.

de Swaan, A. (1998). A political sociology of the world language system: The dynamics of language spread. *Language Problems and Language Planning, 22*(1), 63–75.

de Swaan, A. (2001a). *Words of the world: The global language system.* Polity Press.

de Swaan, A. (2001b). A political sociology of the world language system. In Y. Sternberg & E. Ben-Rafael (eds.), *Identity, culture and globalization* (pp. 205–233). Brill Academic Press.

de Swaan, A. (2002). *The world language system: A political sociology and political economy of language.* Polity Press.

de Swaan, A. (2004). The language constellation of the European Union. In M. Kohli & M. Novak (eds.), *Will Europe work?* (pp. 170–195). Routledge.

Dearing, R., & King, L. (2007). *Languages review.* London: DfES [online]. Accessed 1 August 2013 at www.teachernet.gov.uk/_doc/11124/Language Review.pdf.

Deci, E. L., & Ryan, R. M. (2000). The 'what' and 'why' of goal pursuits: Human needs and the self-determination of behavior. *Psychological Inquiry, 11*(4), 227–268.

Del Percio, A., & Flubacher, M. (2017). Language, education and neoliberalism. In M.-C. Flubacher, & D. Percio (eds.), *Language, education and neoliberalism: Critical studies in sociolinguistics* (pp. 1–18). Multilingual Matters.

Dewaele, J. M. (2018). Why the dichotomy 'L1 versus LX user' is better than 'native versus non-native speaker'. *Applied Linguistics, 39*(2), 236–240.

Dewaele, J.-M., & MacIntyre, P. D. (2016). Foreign language enjoyment and foreign language classroom anxiety: The right and left feet of FL learning? In P. D. MacIntyre, T. Gregersen, & S. Mercer (eds.), *Positive psychology in SLA* (pp. 215–236). Multilingual Matters.

Dickey, E. (2015). Teaching Latin to Greek speakers in antiquity. In E. P. Archibald, W. Brockliss, & J. Gnoza (eds.), *Learning Latin and Greek from antiquity to the present* (Vol. 37; pp. 30–51). Cambridge University Press.

Dörnyei, Z. (2019). Towards a better understanding of the L2 learning experience, the Cinderella of the L2 motivational self system. *Studies in Second Language Learning and Teaching, 9*(1), 19–30.

Dörnyei, Z., & Al-Hoorie, A. H. (2017). The motivational foundation of learning languages other than global English: Theoretical issues and research directions. *The Modern Language Journal, 101*(3), 455–468.

Dörnyei, Z., & Csizér, K. (1998). Ten commandments for motivating language learners: Results of an empirical study. *Language Teaching Research, 2*(3), 203–229.

Dörnyei, Z., & Németh, N. (2006). *Motivation, language attitudes and globalisation: A Hungarian perspective.* Multilingual Matters.

Dörnyei, Z., & Ushioda, E. (2021). *Teaching and researching motivation.* Routledge.

Dörnyei, Z., Henry, A., & Muir, C. (2015). *Motivational currents in language learning: Frameworks for focused interventions.* Routledge.

Duff, P. A. (2017). Commentary: Motivation for learning languages other than English in an English-dominant world. *The Modern Language Journal, 101*(3), 597–607.

East, M. (2021a). Language learning in New Zealand's schools: Enticing opportunities and enduring constraints. In U. Lanvers, A. Thompson, &

M. East (eds.), *Language learning in anglophone countries: Challenges, practices, ways forward* (pp. 19–36). Palgrave.

East, M. (2021b). *Foundational principles of task-based language teaching*. Taylor & Francis.

ECML. (n.d.). *European Centre for Modern Languages of the Council of Europe. Plurilingual and Intercultural Education: Resources.* Accessed 1 August 2023 at https://bit.ly/4ddGYQz.

Ellis, E. M. (2008). Defining and investigating monolingualism. *Sociolinguistic Studies*, *2*(3), 311–330.

Erling, E., & Moore, E. (2021). Socially just plurilingual education in Europe: Shifting subjectivities and practices through research and action. *International Journal of Multilingualism*, *18*(3), 1–11.

Ethnologue. (2019). *22nd ed.* Accessed 18 May 2022 at www.ethnologue.com/ethnoblog/gary-simons/welcome-22nd-edition.

European Commission. (1995). *White paper on education and training teaching and learning: Towards the learning society.* Accessed 1 August 2023 at https://eur-lex.europa.eu/LexUriServ/LexUriServ.do?uri=COM:1995:0590: FIN:EN:PDF.

European Commission. (2015). *Adult education and training in Europe: Programmes to raise achievement in basic skills: Country descriptions.* Accessed 27 May 2022 at https://bit.ly/3UllLu2.

European Parliament. (n.d.). *EU fact sheet on the European Union: Language Policy.* Accessed 10 July 2013 at www.europarl.europa.eu/factsheets/en/sheet/142/language-policy.

Eurostats. (2022). Accessed 1 August 2022 at https://bit.ly/44gmGBT.

Extra, G., & Yagmur, K. (2012). Towards European indicators of language policies and practices. In G. Extra & K. Yagmur (eds.), *Language rich Europe: Trends in policies and practices for multilingualism in Europe* (pp. 13–27). Cambridge University Press.

Fidrmuc, J., & Fidrmuc, J. (2016). Foreign languages and trade: Evidence from a natural experiment. *Empirical Economics*, *50*(1), 31–49.

Fögen, T. (2000). *Patrii sermonis egestas: Einstellungen lateinischer Autoren zu ihrer Muttersprache: ein Beitrag zum Sprachbewußtsein in der römischen Antike*. K. G. Saur.

Forbes, K., Evans, M., Fisher, L., et al. (2021). Developing a multilingual identity in the languages classroom: The influence of an identity-based pedagogical intervention. *Language Learning Journal*, *49*(4), 433–451.

Foreman-Peck, J., & Wang, Y. (2014). The costs to the UK of language deficiencies as a barrier to UK engagement in exporting: A report to UK trade & investment. *Cardiff Business School.* Accessed 10 May 2022 at https://bit.ly/3Qml18i.

Gallagher-Brett, A. (2004). *Seven hundred reasons for studying languages.* University of Southampton. Accessed 15 June 2021 at https://eprints.soton.ac.uk/362669/1/700_reasons.pdf.

Gao, F. (2011). Exploring the reconstruction of Chinese learners' national identities in their English-language-learning journeys in Britain. *Journal of Language, Identity & Education, 10*(5), 287–305.

Gao, F. & Liu, H. (2022). Revisiting students' foreign language learning demotivation: From concepts to themes. *Frontiers in Psychology, 13*, 1030634.

Gao, X., & Lamb, T. (2011). Exploring links between identity, motivation and autonomy. In G. Murray, X. Gao, & T. Lamb (eds.), *Identity, motivation and autonomy in language learning* (pp. 1–8). Multilingual Matters.

Gao, X., & Zheng, Y. (2019). Multilingualism and higher education in Greater China. *Journal of Multilingual and Multicultural Development, 40*(7), 555–561.

García, O., Wei, L., (2014). The translanguaging turn and its impact. In O. García & L. Wei (eds.), *Translanguaging: Language, bilingualism and education* (pp. 19–44). Springer.

García Bermejo, M. L. (2021). Foreign language education in Spain: A historical view. *European Journal of Applied Linguistics, 9*(1), 115–135.

Gardner, R. C. (2010). *Motivation and second language acquisition: The socio-educational model.* Peter Lang.

Garret, P. (2010). *Attitudes to language.* Cambridge University Press.

Gazzola, M. (2016). Multilingual communication for whom? Language policy and fairness in the European Union. *European Union Politics, 17*(4), 546–549.

Gazzola, M. (2023). Language policy as public policy. In M. Gazzola, F. Gobbo, D. Cassels Johnson, & J. A. Leoni de León (eds.), *Epistemological and theoretical foundations in language policy and planning* (pp. 41–71). Palgrave.

Gazzola, M., Gobbo, F., Johnson, D. C., & Leoni de León, J. A. (eds.). (2023). *Epistemological and theoretical foundations in language policy and planning.* Palgrave.

Gilsdorf, J. (2002). Standard Englishes and World Englishes: Living with a polymorph business language. *Journal of Business Communication, 39*, 364–378.

Godrej, F. (2011). Spaces for counter-narratives: The phenomenology of reclamation. *Frontiers: A Journal of Women Studies, 32*(3), 111–133.

Gogolin, I. Hansen, S., McMonagle, Rauch, D. & Leseman, P. (eds.). (2020). *Handbuch Mehrsprachigkeit und Bildung*. Springer.

Graham, S. (2022). Self-efficacy and language learning: What it is and what it isn't. *Language Learning Journal*, *50*(2), 186–207.

Graham, S., & Macaro, E. (2008). Strategy instruction in listening for lower-intermediate learners of French. *Language Learning*, *58*(4), 747–783.

Graham, S., & Santos, D. (2015). Language learning in the public eye: An analysis of newspapers and official documents in England. *Innovation in Language Learning and Teaching*, *9*(1), 72–85.

Graham, S., Woore, R., Porter, A., Courtney, L., & Savory, C. (2020). Navigating the challenges of L2 reading: Self-efficacy, self-regulatory reading strategies, and learner profiles. *Modern Language Journal*, *104*(4), 693–714.

Gramling, D. (2016). *The invention of monolingualism*. Bloomsbury Publishing.

Grin, F. (2008). Principles of policy evaluation and their application to multilingualism in the European Union. In X. Arzoz (ed.), *Respecting linguistic diversity in the European Union* (pp. 73–84). John Benjamins.

Griva, E., Panteli, P., & Nihoritou, I. (2016). Policies for plurilingual education and FL teaching in three European countries: A comparative account of teachers' views. *International Journal of Languages' Education and Teaching*, *4*(2), 37–58.

Gu, M. (2009). *The discursive construction of second language learners' motivation: A multi-level perspective*. Peter Lang.

Haberland, H. (2020). Who profits from Global English? Reply to Hultgren. *Nordic Journal of English Studies*, *19*(3), 143–150.

Hall, E. (1989). *Inventing the barbarian: Greek self-definition through tragedy*. Clarendon Press.

Hawkins, E. (2005). Out of this nettle, drop-out, we pluck this flower, opportunity: Re-thinking the school foreign language apprenticeship. *Language Learning Journal*, *32*(1), 4–17.

Hazel, S. (2016). Why native English speakers fail to be understood in English – and lose out in global business. *The Conversation*. Accessed 20 October 2020 at https://bit.ly/4bfKYhy.

Hélot, C., Frijns, C., Gorp, K., & Sierens, S. (eds.). (2018). *Language awareness in multilingual classrooms in Europe: From theory to practice* (Vol. 109). Walter de Gruyter.

Henry, A. (2010). Contexts of possibility in simultaneous language learning: Using the L2 motivational self system to assess the impact of global English. *Journal of Multilingual and Multicultural Development*, *31*(2), 149–162.

Henry, A. (2012). L3 motivation (Academic thesis, Gotheburg University). Accessed 1 August 2023 at https://bit.ly/4aTywV6.

Henry, A. (2017). Rewarding foreign language learning: Effects of the Swedish grade point average enhancement initiative on students' motivation to learn French. *The Language Learning Journal, 45*(3), 301–315.

Henry, A., & Apelgren, B. M. (2008). Young learners and multilingualism: A study of learner attitudes before and after the introduction of a second foreign language to the curriculum. *System, 36*(4), 607–623.

Henry, A., & Cliffordson, C. (2013). Motivation, gender, and possible selves. *Language Learning, 63*(2), 271–295.

Houghton, S. A., & Hashimoto, K. (2018). *Towards post-native-speakerism*. Nature Singapore.

House, J. (2011). English as a threat to other European languages and European multilingualism? In B. Kortmann & J. van der Auwera (eds.), *The languages and linguistics of Europe* (pp. 591–604). De Gruyter.

Howard, M., & Oakes, L. (2021). Motivation for LOTE learning: A cross-country comparison of university learners of French. *Journal of Multilingual and Multicultural Development, 64*(7), 1–17.

Hu, P., & Zhang, J. (2017). A pathway to learner autonomy: A self-determination theory perspective. *Asia Pacific Education Review, 18*, 147–157.

Huang, H.-T., Hsu, C.-C., & Chen, S.-W. (2015). Identification with social role obligations, possible selves, and L2 motivation in foreign language learning. *System, 51*, 28–38.

Huang, S. C. (2019). Learning experience reigns: Taiwanese learners' motivation in learning eight additional languages as compared to English. *Journal of Multilingual and Multicultural Development, 40*(7), 576–589.

Hult, F. M. (2017). More than a lingua franca: Functions of English in a globalised educational language policy. *Language, Culture and Curriculum, 30*(3), 265–282.

Hultgren, A. K. (2020). Global English: From 'tyrannosaurus rex' to 'red herring'. *Nordic Journal of English Studies, 19*(3), 10–34.

Isaacs, T., & Rose, H. (2021). Redressing the balance in the native speaker debate: Assessment standards, standard language, and exposing double standards. *TESOL Quarterly 56*(1), 401–412.

Jakubiak, C. (2020). 'English is out there – you have to get with the program': Linguistic instrumentalism, global citizenship education, and English-language voluntourism. *Anthropology & Education Quarterly, 51*, 212–232.

Jeffreys, B. (2019). *Language learning: German and French drop by half in UK schools*. BBC News. Accessed 10 November 2023 at www.bbc.co.uk/news/education-47334374.

Jenkins, J. (2017). The future of English as a lingua franca? In J. Jenkins, W. Baker, & M. Dewey (eds.), *The Routledge handbook of English as a lingua franca* (pp. 594–605). Routledge.

Johnson, D. C. (2013). *Language policy*. Palgrave Macmillan.

Johnson, D. C., & Johnson, E. J. (2015). Power and agency in language policy appropriation. *Language Policy, 14*(3), 221–243.

Kachru, B. B. (1992). Teaching world Englishes. In B. Kachru (ed.), *The other tongue: English across cultures*, (pp. 355–365). University of Illinois Press.

Kachru, B. B. (2006). The English language in the outer circle. *World Englishes, 3*, 241–255.

Kanna, A. S., & Rakesh, J. (2023). The role of English education in the development of modern India: A historical and sociocultural analysis. *YMER Digital, 22*(4), 265–276.

Kaplan, R. B., & Baldauf, R. B. (1997). *Language planning from practice to theory*. Multilingual Matters.

Kelly, M., and Jones, D. (2003). *A new landscape for languages*. The Nuffield Foundation.

Kim, T. Y., & Kim, Y. (2021). Structural relationship between L2 learning motivation and resilience and their impact on motivated behavior and L2 proficiency. *Journal of Psycholinguistic Research, 50*, 417–436.

Kioko, A. N., Ndung'u, R. W., Njoroge, M. C., & Mutiga, J. (2014). Mother tongue and education in Africa: Publicising the reality. *Multilingual Education, 4*, 1–11.

Kobayashi, Y. (2013). Europe versus Asia: Foreign language education other than English in Japan's higher education. *Higher Education, 66*, 269–281.

Kong, J. H., Han, J. E., Kim, S., et al. (2018). L2 motivational self-system, international posture and competitiveness of Korean CTL and LCTL college learners: A structural equation modeling approach. *System, 72*, 178–189.

Kouritzin, S. G., Piquemal, N. A., & Renaud, R. D. (2009). An international comparison of socially constructed language learning motivation and beliefs. *Foreign Language Annals, 42*(2), 287–317.

Kramsch, C. (2005). Post 9/11: Foreign languages between knowledge and power. *Applied Linguistics, 26*(4), 545–567.

Kramsch, C. (2014). Teaching foreign languages in an era of globalization: Introduction. *The Modern Language Journal, 98*(1), 296–311.

Krzyżanowski, M., & Wodak, R. (2011). Political strategies and language policies: The European Union Lisbon strategy and its implications for the EU's language and multilingualism policy. *Language Policy, 10*, 115–136.

Lamb, M., Csizér, K., Henry, A., & Ryan, S. (eds.). (2019). *The Palgrave handbook of motivation for language learning*. Palgrave Macmillan.

References

Lanvers, U. (2012). 'The Danish speak so many languages it's really embarrassing'. The impact of L1 English on adult language students' motivation. *Innovation in Language Learning and Teaching, 6*(2), 157–175.

Lanvers, U. (2016a). On the predicaments of the English L 1 language learner: A conceptual article. *International Journal of Applied Linguistics, 26*(2), 147–167.

Lanvers, U. (2016b). Lots of selves, some rebellious: Developing the self-discrepancy model for language learners. *System, 60*, 79–92.

Lanvers, U. (2017a). Contradictory others and the habitus of languages: Surveying the L2 motivation landscape in the United Kingdom. *Modern Language Journal, 101*(3), 517–32.

Lanvers, U. (2017b). Elitism in language learning in the UK. In D. Rivers & K. Kotzmann (eds.), *Isms in language education* (pp. 50–73). De Gruyter.

Lanvers, U. (2018a). Public debates of the Englishization of education in Germany. *European Journal of Language Policy, 10*(1), 39–77.

Lanvers, U. (2018b). 'If they are going to university, they are gonna need a language GCSE': Co-constructing the social divide in language learning in England. *System, 76*, 129–143.

Lanvers, U. (2020). Changing language mindsets about modern languages: A school intervention. *The Language Learning Journal, 48*(5), 571–597.

Lanvers, U. (2021). UK language policy quo vadis? Language learning in the UK post Brexit. In C. Cunningham & C. Hall (eds.), *Vulnerabilities, challenges and risks in applied linguistics* (pp. 97–110). Multilingual Matters.

Lanvers, U. (2024). EU politicians debating European language education policy: Who supports the 1+2 policy? *European Journal of Language Education, 16*(1), 5–26. https://doi.org/10.3828/ejlp.2024.2.

Lanvers, U., & Chambers, G. (2019). In the shadow of global English? Comparing language learner motivation in Germany and the United Kingdom. In M. Lamb, K. Csizér, A. Henry, & S. Ryan (eds.), *The Palgrave handbook of motivation for language learning* (pp. 429–448). Palgrave Macmillan.

Lanvers, U., & Coleman, J. A. (2017). The UK language learning crisis in the public media: A critical analysis. *Language Learning Journal, 45*(1), 3–25.

Lanvers, U., & Graham, S. (2022). Can we design language education policy and curricula for a motivated learner? Self-determination theory and the UK language crisis. *Language Learning Journal, 50*(2), 223–237.

Lanvers, U., Hultgren, K., & Gayton, A. M. (2019). 'People can be smarter with two languages': Changing anglophone students' attitudes to language learning through teaching linguistics. *Language Learning Journal, 47*(1), 88–104.

Lanvers, U., Thompson, A. S., & East, M. (eds.). (2021a). *Language learning in anglophone countries: Challenges, practices, ways forward*. Palgrave.

Lanvers, U., Thompson, A. S., & East, M. (2021b). Introduction: Is language learning in anglophone countries in crisis? In U. Lanvers, A. S. Thompson, & M. East (eds.), *Language learning in anglophone countries: Challenges, practices, ways forward* (pp. 1–15). Palgrave.

Larina, T. V., Sukhanova, A. S., Kodirov, B. R., Kuchinskaya, E. A., & Borisova, E. V. (2020). Students' patriotic values formation by means of a foreign language as an important issue. *PalArch's Journal of Archaeology of Egypt/Egyptology, 17*(3), 347–354.

Lawes, S. (2000). Why learn a foreign language? In K. Field (ed.), *The changing place of modern foreign languages in the curriculum* (pp. 39–50). Issues in Modern Foreign Languages Teaching 1. Routledge.

Leonhardt, J. (2013). *Latin: History of a world language*. Cambridge University Press.

Li, Z., & Liu, Y. (2023). Theorising language learning experience in LOTE motivation with PERMA: A positive psychology perspective. *System, 112*, 1–13.

Liddicoat, J. (eds.). (2022). *Current Issues in Language Planning*. Special Issue 22(5). *Language planning for diversity in language education*.

Liddicoat, A. J. (2022). Language planning for diversity in foreign language education. *Current Issues in Language Planning, 23*(5), 457–465.

Liddicoat, A., & Scarino, A. (2010). *Languages in Australian education: Problems, prospects and future directions*. Cambridge Scholars.

Lin, H. Y. (2013). Critical perspectives on global English: A study of their implications. *Intergrams, 13*(2), 24–22.

Liu, M., & Oga-Baldwin, W. Q. (2022). Motivational profiles of learners of multiple foreign languages: A self-determination theory perspective. *System, 106*, 102762.

LLAS. (n.d.). *Linguistics area studies: Seven hundred reasons for studying languages*. Accessed 10 February 2022 at www.llas.ac.uk/sites/default/files/nodes/6063/700_reasons.pdf.

Lo Bianco, J., & Aronin, L. (2020), *Dominant language constellations*. Springer.

Lo Bianco, J., Slaughter, Y., & Australian Council for Educational Research (ACER). (2009). Second languages and Australian schooling. Accessed 30 April 2024 at https://research.acer.edu.au/aer/8/.

Looney, D., & Lusin, N. (2019). Enrollments in languages other than English in United States institutions of higher education, Summer 2016 and Fall 2016. Accessed 1 August 2023 at https://bit.ly/3UhpE4v.

López, J. S. (2018). The teaching and learning of foreign languages in Spain from the sixteenth to eighteenth centuries: Influences and inter-relationships. *Language Learning Journal, 46*(1), 51–61.

Lu, J., & Shen, Q. (2022). Understanding China's LOTE learners' perceptions and choices of LOTE (s) and English learning: A linguistic market perspective. *Current Issues in Language Planning*, *23*(4), 394–411.

MacIntyre, P. D., Ross, J., & Clément, R. (2019). Emotions are motivating. In M. Lamb, K. Csizér, A. Henry, & S. Ryan (eds.), *The Palgrave handbook of motivation for language learning* (pp. 183–202). Palgrave Macmillan.

Mahmoodi, M. H., & Yousefi, M. (2022). Second language motivation research 2010–2019: A synthetic exploration. *Language Learning Journal*, *50*(3), 273–296.

Martin, P. (2010). 'They have lost their identity but not gained a British one': Non-traditional multilingual students in higher education in the United Kingdom. *Language and Education*, *24*, 9–20.

Mason, S., & Hajek, J. (2021). Language education in Australian primary schools: Policy, practice, perceptions. In U. Lanvers, A. Thompson, & M. East (eds.), *Language learning in anglophone countries: Challenges, practices, ways forward* (pp. 135–153). Palgrave.

May, S. (2019). Negotiating the multilingual turn in SLA. *The Modern Language Journal*, *103*, 122–129.

McEown, M., Sawaki, Y., & Harada, T. (2017). Foreign language learning motivation in the Japanese context: Social and political influences on self. *Modern Language Journal*, *101*(3), 533–547.

McLelland, N. (2018). The history of language learning and teaching in Britain. *The Language Learning Journal*, *46*(1), 6–16.

McWhorter, J. (2011). *The power of Babel: A natural history of language*. Random House.

Mendoza, A., & Phung, H. (2019). Motivation to learn languages other than English: A critical research synthesis. *Foreign Language Annals*, *52*(1), 121–140.

Menken, K., & García, O. (eds.). (2010). *Negotiating language education policies: Educators as policymakers*. Routledge.

Meyer, H. J. (2011). Bologna oder Harvard? Realität und Ideologie bei der deutschen Studienreform. *Zeitschrift für Politik*, *4*, 51–62.

Michel, M., Vidon, C., de Graaff, R., & Lowie, W. (2021). Language learning beyond English in the Netherlands: A fragile future? *European Journal of Applied Linguistics*, *9*(1), 159–182.

Mitchell, R. (2003). Rationales for foreign language education in the 21st century. In S. Sarangi & T. van Leeuwen (eds.), *Applied linguistics and communities of practice* (pp. 14–131). Continuum.

Molla, T., Harvey, A., & Sellar, S. (2019). Access to languages other than English in Australian universities: An educational pipeline of privilege. *Higher Education Research & Development*, *38*(2), 307–323.

Momigliano, A. (1975). The fault of the Greeks. *Daedalus, 102*(4), 9–19.

Muradás-Taylor, B. (2023). Undergraduate language programmes in England: A widening participation crisis. *Arts and Humanities in Higher Education, 22*(3), 322–342.

Nakamura, T. (2019). Understanding motivation for learning languages other than English: Life domains of L2 self. *System, 82*, 111–121.

National K–12 Foreign Language Enrollment Survey Report. (2017). Accessed 10 November 2023 at www.americancouncils.org/sites/default/files/FLE-report-June17.pdf.

Newby, D., Matzer, E., & Penz, H. (2009). *Languages for social cohesion: Language education in a multilingual and multicultural Europe*. Council of Europe.

Noels, K. A., Lou, N. M., Lascano, D. I. V., et al. (2019). Self-determination and motivated engagement in language learning. In M. Lamb, K. Csizér, A. Henry, & S. Ryan (eds.), *The Palgrave handbook of motivation for language learning* (pp. 95–115). Palgrave Macmillan.

Nolan, J. (2019). *The elusive case of lingua franca: Fact and fiction*. Springer.

Oakes, L., & Howard, M. (2022). Learning French as a foreign language in a globalised world: An empirical critique of the L2 motivational self system. *International Journal of Bilingual Education and Bilingualism, 25*(1), 166–182.

O'Malley, J. M., & Chamot, A. U. (1990). *Learning strategies in second language*. Cambridge University Press.

Osborn, T. (2006). *Teaching world languages for social justice: A sourcebook of principles and practices*. Lawrence Erlbaum.

Osler, A. H., & Starkey, H. W. (2015). Education for cosmopolitan citizenship: A framework for language learning. *Argentinian Journal of Applied Linguistics, 3*(2), 30–39.

Osler, A., & Starkey, H. (eds.). (2005). *Citizenship and language learning: International perspectives*. Trentham Books.

Ostler, N. (2005). *Empires of the word: A language history of the world*. Harper Perennial.

Ostler, N. (2010). *The last lingua franca: English until the return of Babel*. Springer.

Oxford, R. L. (2001). 'The bleached bones of a story': Learners' constructions of language teachers. In M. P. Breen (ed.), *Learner contributions to language learning* (pp. 86–111). Longman.

Pachler, N. (2002). Foreign language learning in England in the 21st century. *Language Learning Journal, 25*(1), 4–7.

References

Parrish, A., & Lanvers, U. (2019). Student motivation, school policy choices and modern language study in England. *Language Learning Journal, 47*(3), 281–298.

Pawlak, M. (2022). Making university-level foreign language education more responsive to professional needs. In B. Lewandowska-Tomaszczyk & M. Trojszczak (eds.), *Language use, education, and professional contexts* (pp. 131–142). Springer.

Pennycook, A. (1994). *The cultural politics of English as an international language.* Longman.

Pennycook, A. (2020). The future of Englishes: One, many or none? In A. Kirpatrick (ed.), *The Routledge handbook of world Englishes* (pp. 679–692). Routledge.

Phillipson, R. (1992). *Linguistic imperialism.* Oxford University Press.

Phillipson, R. (2003). *English only Europe?* Routledge.

Phillipson, R. (2017a). Myths and realities of 'global' English. *Language Policy, 16*(3), 313–331.

Philipson, R. (2017b). Myths and realities of European Union language policy. *World Englishes, 36*(3), 347–349.

Phillipson, R., & Skutnabb-Kangas, T. (1996). English only worldwide or language ecology? *TESOL Quarterly, 30*(3), 429–452.

Pintrich, P. R., & Johnson, G. R. (1990). Assessing and improving students' learning strategies. *New Directions for Teaching and Learning,* (42), 83–92.

Pratt, M. L. (2012). 'If English was good enough for Jesus . . .' Monolinguismo y mala fe. *Critical Multilingualism Studies, 1*(1), 12–30.

Ramadhan, S., Sukma, E., & Indriyani, V. (2019). Environmental education and disaster mitigation through language learning. In *IOP conference series: Earth and environmental science, 314*(1), 012054. IOP Publishing.

Raoofi, S., Tan, B. H., & Chan, S. H. (2012). Self-efficacy in second/foreign language learning contexts. *English Language Teaching, 5*(11), 60–73.

Reagan, T., & Osborn, T. A. (2019). Time for a paradigm shift in US foreign language education? In D. Macedo (ed.), *Decolonizing foreign language education: The misteaching of English and other colonial languages* (pp. 73–110). Taylor Francis.

Reinders, H. (2010). Towards a classroom pedagogy for learner autonomy: A framework of independent language learning skills. *Australian Journal of Teacher Education (Online), 35*(5), 40–55.

Rhodes, N. C., & Pufahl, I. (2010). *Foreign language teaching in US schools: Results of a national survey.* Washington, DC. Wiley.

Rhodes, N., & Pufahl, I. (2014). An overview of Spanish teaching in US Schools: National survey results. *Informes del Observatorio/Observatorio Reports*. Instituto Cervantes at FAS Harvard University.

Ricento, T. K., & Hornberger, N. H. (1996). Unpeeling the onion: Language planning and policy and the ELT professional. *TESOL Quarterly, 30*(3), 401–427.

Rivers, D. J. (2011). Japanese national identification and English language learning processes. *International Journal of Intercultural Relations, 35*(1), 111–123.

Rose, H., & Carson, L. (eds.). (2014). *Language Learning in Higher Education* Special Issue *4*(2).

Rose, H., & Galloway, N. (2017). Debating standard language ideology in the classroom: Using the 'speak good English movement' to raise awareness of global Englishes. *Regional Language Centre Journal, 48*(3), 294–301.

Rubio, F. (2018). Language education in elementary schools: Meeting the needs of the nation. *Foreign Language Annals, 51*(1), 90–103.

Ryan, R. M., & Deci, E. L. (2017). *Self-determination theory: Basic psychological needs in motivation, development, and wellness*. Guilford Publications.

Rydenvald, M. (2015). Elite bilingualism? Language use among multilingual teenagers of Swedish background in European schools and international schools in Europe. *Journal of Research in International Education, 14*(3), 213–227.

Schendl, H. (2012). Multilingualism, code-switching, and language contact in historical sociolinguistics. In J. M. Hernández-Campoy & J. C. Conde-Silvestre (eds.), *The handbook of historical sociolinguistics* (pp. 520–533). Blackwell.

Schroedler, T. (2018). The value of foreign language skills in international business for native English speaking countries: A study on Ireland. In T. Sherman & J. Nekvapil (eds.), *English in Business and Commerce: Interactions and Policies* (pp. 231–255). De Gruyter.

Schwan, A. (2021). Perceptions of student motivation and amotivation. *The Clearing House: A Journal of Educational Strategies, Issues and Ideas, 94*(2), 76–82.

SCILT. (n.d.). Accessed 10 December 2023 at https://bit.ly/4deEC3X.

Seargeant, P. (2010). Naming and defining in world Englishes. *World Englishes, 29*(1), 97–113.

Seidelhofer, B. (2005). Habeas corpus and divide et impera: 'Global English' and applied linguistics. In K. Miller & P. Thomson (eds.), *Unity and diversity in language use* (pp. 198–220). Continuum.

References

Shears, M. (2017). *Internet society global internet report 2017: Paths to our digital future*. APO report. Accessed 1 August 2023 at https://apo.org.au/sites/default/files/resource-files/2017-09/apo-nid221186.pdf.

Shohamy, E. (2016). *Language policy: Hidden agendas and new approaches*. Routledge.

Siridetkoon, P. (2015). Motivation, anxiety and international posture of multiple language learners in Thailand (Doctoral dissertation, Birkbeck, University of London).

Skutnabb-Kangas, T. (1996). Educational language choice: Multilingual diversity or monolingual reductionism? In M. Hellinger & U. Ammon (eds.), *Contrastive sociolinguistics*. (pp. 175–204). Mouton de Gruyter.

Skutnabb-Kangas, T., & Phillipson, R. (1996). Linguicide and linguicism. *Contact Linguistics: An International Handbook of Contemporary Research*, *1*, 667–675.

Sockett, G. (2014). *The online informal learning of English*. Springer.

Spiegel, der. (2007). Accessed 1 August 2023 at https://bit.ly/4bfMgJq.

Spiegel, der. (2023). Accessed 10 November 2023 at https://bit.ly/3xTsTHQ.

Spolsky, B. (2019). A modified and enriched theory of language policy (and management). *Language Policy*, *18*(3), 323–338.

Statistics Canada. (2023). English–French bilingualism in Canada. Accessed 10 November 2023 at https://bit.ly/4aULrWD.

Stolte, R. (2015). German language learning in England: Understanding the enthusiasts (Doctoral dissertation, University of Southampton).

Subtirelu, N. C., & Lindemann, S. (2016). Teaching first language speakers to communicate across linguistic difference: Addressing attitudes, comprehension, and strategies. *Applied Linguistics*, *37*(6), 765–783.

Sugita McEown, M., Sawaki, Y., & Harada, T. (2017). Foreign language learning motivation in the Japanese context: Social and political influences on self. *Modern Language Journal*, *101*(3), 533–547.

Taylor, F., & Marsden, E. J. (2014). Perceptions, attitudes, and choosing to study foreign languages in England: An experimental intervention. *Modern Language Journal*, *98*(4), 902–920.

Thompson, A. S. (2017). Language learning motivation in the United States: An examination of language choice and multilingualism. *Modern Language Journal*, *101*(3), 483–500.

Thompson, A. S. (2021). LOTEs in US universities: Benefits, trends, motivations, and opportunities. In U. Lanvers, A. Thomson, & M. East (eds.), *Language learning in Anglophone countries: Challenges, practices, ways forward* (pp. 181–204). Palgrave.

Thompson, A. S., & Liu, Y. (2018). Multilingualism and emergent selves: Context, languages, and the anti-ought-to self. *International Journal of Bilingual Education and Bilingualism, 24*(2), 173–190.

Thompson, A. S., & Vásquez, C. (2015). Exploring motivational profiles through language learning narratives. *Modern Language Journal, 99*(1), 158–174.

Thorner, N., & Kikuchi, K. (2019). The process of demotivation in language learning: An integrative account. In M. Lamb, K. Csizér, A. Henry, & S. Ryan (eds.), *The Palgrave handbook of motivation for language learning* (pp. 367–388). Palgrave Macmillan.

Tollefson, J. W. (1991). *Planning language, planning inequality*. Longman.

Trim, J. L. M. (2002). *Modern languages in the Council of Europe: 1954–1997*. Council of Europe.

UNESCO. (n.d.). Universal Declaration of Human Rights. UDHR. Accessed 1 August 2023 at www.un.org/en/about-us/universal-declaration-of-human-rights.

Ushioda, E. (2012). Motivation: L2 learning as a special case? In S. Mercer, S. Ryan, & M. Williams (eds.), *Psychology for language learning: Insights from research, theory and practice* (pp. 58–73). Springer.

Ushioda, E. (2017). The impact of global English on motivation to learn other languages: Toward an ideal multilingual self. *Modern Language Journal, 101*(3), 469–482.

Ushioda, E., & Dörnyei, Z. (eds.). (2017). *Modern Language Journal*. Special Edition *101*(3), Motivation for languages other than English.

Vallerand, R. J., & Ratelle, C. F. (2002). Intrinsic and extrinsic motivation: A hierarchical model. In E. L. Deci & R. M. Ryan (eds.), *Handbook of self-determination research* (pp. 50–63). University of Rochester Press.

Van Parijs, P. (2020). Linguistic injustice for the sake of greater social justice: A response to Anna Kristina Hultgren. *Nordic Journal of English Studies, 19*(3), 175–178.

Vandergrift, L. (2005). Relationships among motivation orientations, metacognitive awareness and proficiency in L2 listening. *Applied Linguistics, 26*(1), 70–89.

Wang, T. (2023). An exploratory motivational intervention on the construction of Chinese undergraduates' ideal LOTE and multilingual selves: The role of near peer role modeling. *Language Teaching Research, 27*(2), 441–465.

Wei, L. (2018). Translanguaging as a practical theory of language. *Applied Linguistics, 39*(1), 9–30.

Wei, L. (2020). Multilingual English users' linguistic innovation. *World Englishes, 39*(2), 236–248.

Wiley, T. G. (2007). The foreign language 'crisis' in the United States: Are heritage and community languages the remedy? *Critical Inquiry in Language Studies, 4*(2–3), 179–205.

Wilkinson, R., & Gabriëls, R. (eds.). (2021a). *The Englishization of higher education in Europe*. Amsterdam University Press.

Wilkinson, R., & Gabriëls, R. (2021b). Introduction. In R. Wilkinson & R. Gabriëls (eds.), *The Englishization of higher education in Europe* (pp. 11–36). Amsterdam University Press.

Williams, K. (2001). Towards a rationale for foreign language education: Re-stating my reservations. *Language Learning Journal, 24*(1), 43–47.

Williams, M., Burden, R., & Lanvers, U. (2002). 'French is the language of love and stuff': Student perceptions of issues related to motivation in learning a foreign language. *British Educational Research Journal, 28*(4), 503–528.

Wright, S. (2009). The elephant in the room: Language issues in the European Union. *European Journal of Language Policy, 1*(2), 93–120.

Xu, C., & Chen, C. A. (2016). Moving from public service motivation (PSM) to motivation for public service (MPS): Through the lens of self-determination theory. In S. Wade (ed.), *Self-determination theory (SDT): Perspective, applications and impact* (pp. 1–8). Nova Science.

Yashima, T. (2002). Willingness to communicate in a second language: The Japanese EFL context. *Modern Language Journal, 86*(1), 54–66.

Zhang, Q. M., & Kim, T. Y. (2013). Cross-grade analysis of Chinese students' English learning motivation: A mixed-methods study. *Asia Pacific Education Review, 14*, 615–627.

Zheng, Y., Lu, X., & Ren, W. (2019). Profiling Chinese university students' motivation to learn multiple languages. *Journal of Multilingual and Multicultural Development, 40*(7), 590–604.

Acknowledgements

I thank Tetyana Lunyova and David Cowing as well as the anonymous reviewers for their insightful comments on earlier versions of this Element.

I thank my many students over the years for the insight they gave me into learner motivation.

I am grateful to Professor David Cowling for his insights into the topic discussed in Section 1.6.

To David, my most critical, ardent and passionate reader

Cambridge Elements⁼

Language Teaching

Heath Rose
University of Oxford

Heath Rose is Professor of Applied Linguistics and Deputy Director (People) of the Department of Education. Before moving into academia, Heath worked as a language teacher in Australia and Japan in both school and university contexts. He is author of numerous books, such as *Introducing Global Englishes, The Japanese Writing System, Data Collection Research Methods in Applied Linguistics,* and *Global Englishes for Language Teaching.*

Jim McKinley
University College London

Jim McKinley is Professor of Applied Linguistics at IOE Faculty of Education and Society, University College London. He has taught in higher education in the UK, Japan, Australia, and Uganda, as well as US schools. His research targets implications of globalization for L2 writing, language education, and higher education studies, particularly the teaching-research nexus and English medium instruction. Jim is co-author and co-editor of several books on research methods in applied linguistics. He is an Editor-in-Chief of the journal *System*.

Advisory Board

Gary Barkhuizen, *University of Auckland*
Marta Gonzalez-Lloret, *University of Hawaii*
Li Wei, *UCL Institute of Education*
Victoria Murphy, *University of Oxford*
Brian Paltridge, *University of Sydney*
Diane Pecorari, *Leeds University*
Christa Van der Walt, *Stellenbosch University*
Yongyan Zheng, *Fudan University*

About the Series

This Elements series aims to close the gap between researchers and practitioners by allying research with language teaching practices, in its exploration of research informed teaching, and teaching informed research. The series builds upon a rich history of pedagogical research in its exploration of new insights within the field of language teaching.

Cambridge Elements

Language Teaching

Elements in the Series

Intercultural and Transcultural Awareness in Language Teaching
Will Baker

Technology and Language Teaching
Ursula Stickler

Reflective Practice in Language Teaching
Thomas S. C. Farrell

English-Medium Instruction in Higher Education
David Lasagabaster

Task-Based Language Teaching
Daniel O. Jackson

Mediating Innovation through Language Teacher Education
Martin East

Teaching Young Multilingual Learners: Key Issues and New Insights
Luciana C. de Oliveira and Loren Jones

Teaching English as an International Language
Ali Fuad Selvi, Nicola Galloway, and Heath Rose

Peer Assessment in Writing Instruction
Shulin Yu

Assessment for Language Teaching
Aek Phakiti and Constant Leung

Sociocultural Theory and Second Language Developmental Education
Matthew E. Poehner and James P. Lantolf

Language Learning beyond English: Learner Motivation in the Twenty-First Century
Ursula Lanvers

A full series listing is available at: www.cambridge.org/ELAT

For EU product safety concerns, contact us at Calle de José Abascal, 56–1°, 28003 Madrid, Spain or eugpsr@cambridge.org.

www.ingramcontent.com/pod-product-compliance
Lightning Source LLC
LaVergne TN
LVHW020350260326
834688LV00045B/1638